To Evelyn Handler,
President, University of New Hamp

with good wishes.

Stuart Palmer

Stuart Palmer, Ph.D., is Professor and Chairman, Department of Sociology and Anthropology, University of New Hampshire. He is the author of numerous articles and ten books on stress and crime, and he is currently directing research projects on stress and crime and on role relationships among mentally ill persons.

ROLE STRESS

How to Handle
Everyday Tension

Stuart Palmer

A SPECTRUM BOOK

Prentice-Hall, Inc., Englewood Cliffs, N.J. 07632

Library of Congress Cataloging in Publication Data

Palmer, Stuart Hunter   (date)
    Role stress.

    (A Spectrum Book)
    Bibliography: p.
    Includes index.
    1. Stress (Psychology).   2. Social role.
I. Title.
BF575.S75PS7   158'.1   81-4332
ISBN 0-13-782516-1   AACR2
ISBN 0-13-782508-0 (pbk.)

This Spectrum Book can be made available to businesses
and organizations at a special discount when ordered in large
quantities. For more information, contact:
Prentice-Hall, Inc.
General Book Marketing
Special Sales Division
Englewood Cliffs, N.J. 07632

To Anne and Cathy

10 9 8 7 6 5 4 3 2 1

Editorial/production supervision
and interior design by Alberta Boddy
Cover design by Velthaus+King
Manufacturing buyer: Barbara A. Frick

Prentice-Hall International, Inc., *London*
Prentice-Hall of Australia Pty. Limited, *Sydney*
Prentice-Hall of Canada, Ltd., *Toronto*
Prentice-Hall of India Private Limited, *New Delhi*
Prentice-Hall of Japan, Inc., *Tokyo*
Prentice-Hall of Southeast Asia Pte. Ltd., *Singapore*
Whitehall Books Limited, *Wellington, New Zealand*

Contents

v

Preface

What we are and most of what we do are results of the roles we carry out in everyday life. We think we exist apart from these roles, but in large measure we are wrong. Take away our age and sex roles, our racial, ethnic, and social class roles, our work, educational, and religious roles, our community roles, and what would be left of us? Roles prescribe the general outlines of how we are to act in different types of situations. Abolish roles and life would be chaos. Roles help to provide individual identity and group organization. They lend a measure of predictability to life. We expect one another to follow role prescriptions in given types of situations, and for the most part we do. Think of the billions of human situations around the globe—people coming together for this or that purpose, interacting, moving apart. In the main, these episodes of interaction go amazingly smoothly, predictably. Why? The roles we play.

It is because roles provide identity, group organization, and predictability that we have become so dependent on them—overly dependent on them, actually. We do not know how to function without them. We have very nearly become role-bound. We act as if most of our roles did not exist because we want to deny our dependence on them. We talk about how individualistic we are while going right on playing out our roles according to custom.

Because roles prescribe what we are expected to do in various situations, they necessarily curb our natural inclinations. They especially hamper our tendencies to explore, to experiment, to innovate, to be creative. They depress our creativity. Of course, some of this is necessary. If we all followed our inclinations, life would be a madhouse. But the balance has swung very far in the direction of curbing our individuality, our need for self-expression, in favor of smoothly functioning interaction.

Watch how we are forever expecting one another to act in certain ways under given circumstances, even about the most minor and unimportant matters. Observe how upset and angry we become when others fail to do as we expect. Breaches of etiquette are good examples. The use of a profane word, a belch, a button undone—these things under the "wrong" circumstances can be the cause of much consternation and for the actor can be ruinous.

The costs of putting role playing so far ahead of individuality and of self-expression are very great. Much of the stress we experience comes from roles that conflict, that are overdemanding or underdemanding and boring, or that are especially restrictive, such as bureaucratic roles. Stress also comes from being rejected in our roles, from having our roles—our social territories—encroached upon by others, from having to learn certain new roles, and from losing old ones.

We learn to try to measure up to our role demands. From birth onward others reward us for doing so and punish us for failing to do so. Hence, we experience anxiety when for any reason we cannot measure up or fear that we will be unable to do so. Role stress results when our efforts to cope with our role problems do not resolve the problems. Sustained stress causes behavioral difficulties and illness. Much of our physical and mental illness is the result of our inability to cope effectively with persistent role problems.

Learning to cope more effectively with the role stresses of everyday life is something from which we can all profit. This does not necessarily mean simply adjusting ourselves to fit in to our role demands. We do not have to accept our roles passively. Roles can be changed, modified, discarded; exciting and rewarding new roles can be taken on. What is required is a clear understanding of how roles operate, how they affect us, how they cause stress, and how we can learn to innovate constructive role change and ways of coping with role stress. That is what this book is about.

I

THE NATURE OF ROLE STRESS

1

The Power of Roles

THE PERVASIVENESS OF ROLES

Most of our behavior day-in and day-out in every society around the world is role behavior. We move from situation to situation over the day, over the years, carrying out one role and then another. Suppose one were able to fly slowly around the world, hovering at all points of human habitation. One would see four billion of us working, loving, traveling, idling, fighting, playing, sleeping, eating, praying. One would soon notice, after a time, that most behavior of humans in groups is extremely well organized; interaction among people runs, for the most part, very smoothly. This is as true in the African bush as it is in the urban areas of densest population.

People go to work in large factories or on isolated farms. They walk along jungle paths and drive along crowded freeways. They attend and teach in one room and in large centralized schools. They live in nuclear or extended families. They play and watch games of all sorts. To be sure, there are occasional contretemps, mix-ups. People may attack one another, or deviate in other ways. Even then they are likely to follow out roles, but roles that are deviant. The vast majority of the time things go more or less as they are "supposed to." The proportion of the billions of daily interactions that go smoothly far outweighs those that do not.

This is not mainly due to inherited behavioral dispositions; it is not largely due to personality factors. Both of these may play some part, but human organization is in the main due to the fact that each society has a social system—a highly complex body of interrelated social roles. We learn these roles and we carry them out. This is centrally what makes human social life, as we know it, possible.

The idea that we play—carry out—roles makes some of us uncomfortable. It can imply that we are robots, conditioned to follow patterns programmed by some gargantuan entity, the "system" or "society." For others of us, carrying out a role connotes insincerity—a staged performance. These fears mask the reality that we all move in and out of various roles as we go from one social situation to the next. In our waking lives, for the most part, we act in accordance with what others expect of us in given roles. True, we run the risk of becoming role-playing automatons serving the organizational needs of the group. An enormous problem in human life is that all too often we have, in fact, become role bound. At the same time, many roles allow for a good deal of individual expression. The great need is to balance the organizational needs of the human group with the expressive, personal needs of the individual. When we do not achieve this balance, severe problems result.

DEFINING ROLES

We all have sex, age, and family roles. Most of us have work roles. At one time or another, many of us have educational, political, and religious roles. We have recreational roles and roles in community organizations. Finally, we have social class, ethnic, and racial roles. Our complement of roles will, of course, change over time. We take on new roles and shed old ones. Others are modified over the years.

Social roles are made up of patterns of behavior that others expect us to carry out when we occupy certain positions in society. Those others reward us through social approval, personal warmth, and material means when we meet their expectations for our roles. They tend to withhold rewards and, in subtle or direct ways, to punish us when we fail to meet expectations. It is essentially because of these rewards and punishments that we learn to carry out our roles adequately. That is, we learn to conform to commonly held expectations as to how we should act under certain circumstances.

Each of us is an individual with a body, genetic heritage, and social experience in some way unique. All of us need room to meet our individual needs, to express ourselves creatively. It is true that others seldom demand that we exactly meet role expectations. Some tolerance is usually made for our individual way of doing things. Some, but not much. The problem is not that we are solely mechanical role players, but rather that we are in danger of becoming so. All too often our roles work against our needs, forcing us to behave in quite rigidly patterned ways—at the expense of our individuality.

As an example of the pervasiveness of roles in our lives, look at the concerns of the feminist movement of today. Those concerns are centrally about the female role in relation to the male role. The thrust of the movement is to bring about symmetry between the two roles, to remove the power imbalances that entrenched role expectations create. The macho, ultracompetitive male role and the passive, relatively uncompetitive female role are increasingly seen to be harmful to all.

A second example has to do with age roles. The young bridle at expectations that restrict their natural tendencies to explore and to test reality. The elderly resent an age role thrust upon them by others whose expectations, if followed, relegate them to the far sidelines of life. The crisis of middle age is brought about, in good measure, by attempts to adjust to changing age role expectations, especially those that demand that full, vigorous participation in social life be replaced by a passive acceptance of the transition to the elderly role.

A third example is in the realm of work. For most humans, work is an important element of life. Many complain about their jobs, but few would give up work entirely. It can be a way of expressing oneself, of achieving much psychological, as well as material, reward. Work can also, however, be annoying, harmful, and debilitating. The major complaints and the unhappiness of workers center around occupational role expectations that seem to them unsuitable. Work roles may demand more in time, energy, and ability than individuals can provide. They may be undemanding, so much so that they present no challenge and engender painful boredom. They may make contradictory or conflicting demands. Again, they may be especially restrictive, limiting one's natural inclinations unduly.

ROLES MAKE LIFE PREDICTABLE

Roles are the main mechanisms by which we organize ourselves into groups, societies. We are social creatures. We can exist only in groups, not alone. We have few instincts to bind us together as do lower animals. Hence, we have developed gigantic social systems that are the organizational backbones of societies. These are exceedingly intricate systems of thousands upon thousands of interrelated social roles. We take them for granted. We overlook the fact that social systems are man's greatest achievements, far more complex than any of our technological developments.

Social roles specify the nature of interaction between people occupying different positions in social situations. A role is always carried out vis-à-vis one or more other roles. There are no wives without husbands, no parents without sons or daughters, no teachers without students, and vice versa in each case.

Above all, roles make it possible to predict one another's behavior in given types of situations. As we move in one specific situation and then another, we predict in broad outline what others will do. They predict what we will do. We act on our mutual predictions. Our behaviors validate one another's predictions. You drive down the street, predicting that others will also drive on the right. They predict that you will. You go in a store where you, the other customers, and the clerks are all predicting what one another will do. You attend a conference in a foreign country: The biggest mix-up is that you get a room without a bath. Many of those directly interacting with one another have never even met before. Amazing when you think about it, especially when you consider that this gigantic system of organization is not, certainly not predominantly, based on inborn behavior patterns. It is in the main not even grounded in the formal training of individuals. It is due largely to an exceedingly complicated system of role learning that goes on day-in and day-out in every family, every school, every work place, and every community.

Without social roles there would be little predictability in human affairs and no group organization. It is the need for predictability as the basis of social organization that makes us become upset, annoyed, and angry when people deviate, especially unexpectedly, from role behavior. Such deviation threatens us, because it threatens group organization—threatens the very basis of social life upon which we are dependent for our existence.

We humans have never evolved another way nearly as effectively as social roles for achieving and maintaining group organization. Roles work. Thus, we have become dependent on them—too much so—overdependent on them, really. We become threatened even by the most minor deviation from role behavior by others, thereby choking off creative, inventive behavior. In our excessive desire to maintain a sense of predictability and therefore to perpetuate group organization, we have gone to extremes. We have become role bound.

LEARNING ROLES

We are trained from infancy onward to fit into, to carry out, and to conform to a wide variety of social roles. Children are naturally curious, exploratory, and creative creatures. They like to try out this and that way of responding to various situations and problems. In our rush to make competent role players of our children, we stamp out—to far too great an extent—this exploratory drive. This is harmful to the society, since a major source of creative change is stifled. It is also harmful to the children, because their capacity for self-expression and individuality is stunted.

In our desire to make "acceptable" and "responsible" adults out of our children, we all too often succeed in making of them role-playing robots. We tell small children in the home what to do under given conditions. We act as role models, showing them what to do and how to do it. We reward them with approval, warmth, affection, and material things for compliance. We punish them with disapproval, coldness, lack of affection, and withdrawal of material rewards for deviation. The schools continue the process. So do the wider community and the work place when the children become adults.

To be sure, children need guidelines, need very much to learn the basic rules of life, and need to learn to be cooperating, caring individuals. Otherwise, social life would be chaos. The problem is one of balance between individual and social needs. The most minor transgressions by children and adults as well—lapses in etiquette, for example—often trigger concern, alarm, and even aggression. In our zeal to insure predictability, we are prone to take away individuality.

Some children react to undue pressure to conform to the demands of sex roles, age roles, and student roles with rebellious delinquent acts, anxiety symptoms, and physical aggression and resort to drugs and alcohol for escape. We drive them to the very behavior we are so concerned to have them avoid.

Individuals thus develop into adults with personalities far too dependent on role success as it is measured by others. Personal identity becomes based in great degree on role-playing abilities, on whether others approve or disapprove of performance in one role, then another. At the same time, we still have that side to us that longs for the opportunity to express ourselves as unique persons, to be creative and innovative. This conflict between the need to be an individual and the social pressures to be conforming units in the social machine is at the heart of many of our most severe problems.

Even with our overemphasis on role conformity, it is obvious that different people behave somewhat differently in the same role. All fathers are not the same, all six-year-old girls are not the same, all lawyers are not the same. This is in part because there are variations in the content of many roles, depending on social class, ethnic groupings, and regional settings. Parents in the various classes, ethnic groups, and sections of the country train their children somewhat differently in sex, age, and other roles. Occupations have slightly different flavors in different settings.

Within class, ethnic, and regional groups, there are, of course, distinct differences among individuals in how they carry out the same roles. They have not had identical training; their role learning experiences have not all been precisely the same. However, most of us are conditioned to do much the same things over and over under given social conditions. What we do is likely to fit within the tolerance limits of expectations for a particular role.

We may behave a little differently than others who carry out the same role. Styles of role playing vary somewhat from one person to another, but how any one of us acts out a given role usually changes but little from one day to the next. This is in part because our way of performing the role is probably more comfortable, at least in the short run, than any other. It is also because others come to expect us to be consistent in our personal way of carrying out a role. If we must be a little different, they in effect say that at least we should be predictably so. We tend to reward one another for that and to withhold reward or to punish for inconsistency.

As has been emphasized, some fair measure of consistency and conformity in role playing is necessary if we are to be organized into societies, and that we must be if we are to avoid daily chaos and survive. However, the pendulum has swung toward the extreme of obliteration of personal identity as the cost of conformity. To repeat: The great need is to learn how to manage our roles so that we strike a constructive balance between self and society. If we do not, the consequence can be stress that is increasingly debilitating.

THE COMPLEXITY OF ROLE PLAYING

Almost everyone on earth is involved every day in learning roles and in shifting from one role to another—husband or wife, parent, son or daughter, worker (often a boss and a subordinate at the same time), student, community organization member, or religious person. This takes extraordinary learning and skill. Most of us do this so well that we fail utterly to realize how complex our behavior is. If someone invented a machine, a robot, that had one thousandth of the social skills that man has we would think it the greatest invention of all time. However, when we ourselves carry out these thousands upon thousands of complicated interactions daily and do it smoothly, we think little of it. The computers we now have do essentially one thing—they calculate very rapidly, much more rapidly than humans. However, that is about all they do. Also, of course, humans have to feed instructions into them to enable them to do that. The most advanced computer is very, very simple compared to the human brain. The individuals we label as mentally deficient have brains enormously more complex than any computer. Yet we revere the computer, stand in awe of it. We put it on a pedestal, literally with velvet ropes surrounding the area, with humidity and temperature carefully controlled. Often the men and women who program the computer work in far less comfortable quarters.

We give little credit to ourselves, then, for our vast array of social skills, for our ability to play a wide variety of roles, and for our ability to switch from one role to another smoothly and for the most part unerringly. We do, however, fixate upon, give attention to, our "mistakes"—our failures to carry out even minute aspects of our roles properly, according to the expectations of others. A few spots of soup on the tie, a mispronounced word, a grimace, a belch, a few buttons undone, a wink, an obscenity or two—these at the "wrong" times can quickly lead to the view that a person is inept, unpredictable, or unsuitable for serious participation in certain situations. Repeated frequently, in especially inappropriate settings, they can lead to a conception of one as strange or unbalanced.

The fact that we grow so concerned over minor deviations from role expectations shows how critical—how important—roles are in our lives. Interrelated roles and their attendant expectations constitute the fabric of a society. Deviations from them, except under certain specified conditions, cause rents in the social fabric. Our predictions of what one another will do begin to break down. We feel threatened. We grow apprehensive. We become angry. We take action to correct the inappropriate behavior of others.

DEVIANT ROLES

When we speak of conformity, we are referring to behavior that closely follows role expectations. The more behavior diverges from those expectations, the more it is deviant. Generally speaking, deviant behavior is socially disapproved because it is likely to disrupt the ordinary predictable flow of interaction. There are exceptions. Advances in science and the arts are necessary forms of deviance. If the scientist or the artist strictly followed routine behavior patterns, there would be no scientific breakthroughs, no artistic creativity. Innovation, creative work, necessarily diverges from common expectations and so is a form of deviance.

Most forms of deviance, however, are devalued by society and attempts, small or large, are made to punish those who carry them out.

Minor deviations are likely to put one in the nuisance category. Larger ones, especially those having to do with violence or theft, lead to the labeling of the person as criminal. Still other forms cause the individual to be diagnosed as mentally ill. Broadly speaking, behavior that is decidedly inappropriate to a role situation, but does not threaten others' physical well-being or property, is likely to qualify one for the designation of mentally ill person: talking to God in a restaurant, refusing to talk to anyone, or talking to just about everyone.

There are, to be sure, mentally ill persons who do not behave in an outwardly deviant fashion. They experience excruciating anxiety and need continual medical or psychological help, or both. If they are in a mental hospital for a considerable length of time, however, they are likely to begin to behave outwardly in one or more deviant ways. This is because they are expected to take on the role of a mental hospital patient. As such, they are expected to act peculiarly. The other patients do. Gradually, they learn to act as mental patients *should* act—they learn the role of the mental hospital patient.

This illustrates the point that deviant roles develop and are carried out by individuals, as are conforming roles. The difference is that most deviant roles are negatively evaluated by the overall society. Playing a deviant role properly means conforming to expectations that one will act predictably in socially disapproved ways. To use what at first glance seems like double talk, the individual will be rewarded—approved of—for acting in ways that later bring him disapproval and other punishments. If the mental patient behaves as a mental patient is expected to, then the hospital personnel say he or she is making improvement. If the patient refuses to do so, they say he or she is getting sicker. The patient is rewarded for acting in ways that then bring stigma from the wider society.

The people who make the initial determination that a person is deviant—psychiatrists, police officers, judges, teachers, and so forth—tend to have a vested interest in seeing their judgment validated. The person who refuses "to go along" throws their professional judgment into serious question.

There are two other especially important reasons why a society tolerates—in fact, brings about—deviant roles of which it disapproves. Channeling what would otherwise be idiosyncratic deviance—that is, divergence from the usual social roles—into routinized role behavior makes deviance more predictable and less disruptive. Secondly, the deviant roles and the deviants really strengthen the socially acceptable roles and the place of conformists in society. For it is only by the existence of deviant roles and deviant individuals that the nature and "value" of socially acceptable roles and conforming individuals can be clearly understood.

THE POWER OF ROLES

Anyone who is dubious about the great power of roles in our lives can readily enough become a believer in their pervasive influence. All that is necessary is to go out of role, to depart quite definitely from the role one is expected to play in a given type of situation. One sociologist has his students play a role other than son or daughter when they go home to visit their parents during vacation. They play the role of acquaintance invited to spend the weekend. Most are able to do this readily enough. They show a detached formality that is taken for granted when displayed by house guests but is jarringly incongruous for sons and daughters. The consternation of the parents is marked. Some fear their offspring have suffered a mental breakdown.

Role confusion by an individual also illustrates the power of roles in everyday life. A retired business executive enrolled in a graduate program in economics at a well-known university. He persisted in taking the role of the professor in his various courses. He felt, because of his vast experience, more qualified to teach than the graduate faculty. The classes became disorganized. He was asked by the associate dean to withdraw from graduate school. He refused. There was general agreement that he was senile, but how to get rid of him? Finally, an offer was made to allow him to teach an evening division course to undergraduates, providing he withdrew from the graduate courses. After much discussion and "negotiation," he agreed. The associate dean then arranged things so that very few students enrolled for the undergraduate course. According to common practice, it was then cancelled.

A young man decided that female clothes were more comfortable than male attire and decided to dress as a woman. He gained considerable notoriety and eventually appeared on a television talk show wearing a blouse and skirt. He said he was not a transvestite, but was heterosexual. He had always liked to wear women's clothes, he said; they felt better, airier, and more comfortable. As a teen-ager he did not do so because of the fear of being ridiculed. Now in his twenties, he wore women's clothes every day. Why shouldn't he, he asked; women wore men's trousers and no one was bothered. His girl friend did not mind, but in general people reacted with hostility. It was very difficult to get a job, he explained. He had applied for a job as a telephone operator. The company personnel officer said he must dress in men's clothes. The customers could not see him, he replied. Someone might come in and see him, he was told. He was turned down for the job. He applied to do volunteer work with the blind. Fine, as long as he wore men's clothes, a social worker told him. The blind would not see him, he said. That was worse still, the social worker answered. There he would be, going among the blind in women's clothes and they would not even know he was in their midst. He was rejected for the unpaid, volunteer work.

Accounts have been written, of course, about two people switching roles for a period. There are also many reports of individuals who have, unknown to others, taken on roles strange to them—not as imposters in the usual sense but rather for "experimental" purposes. Criminal court judges have been "sentenced" to prison and sociologists and others have been "committed" to mental institutions for short periods. A journalist spent months traveling through the South as a migrant black worker.

The reports all have one thing in common: It is an exceedingly stressful experience. Simply trying to carry out the expected behaviors is extremely wearing. In cases where the person's true identity is hidden, there is the necessity to cover up any indications of the old roles while performing the new ones. In most of these instances there is also the additional strain of being in a deviant role that is received with disapproval and where some form of coercive "treatment" is involved.

From another perspective, certain of these role experiments illustrate the difficulty of attempting to rid oneself of a deviant role. Three men were admitted to a mental hospital as extreme paranoid cases. They were psychiatrically diagnosed as such. Soon after admission, each protested that he was perfectly sane and proceeded to attempt to demonstrate that by acting as he normally did. In each instance hospital personnel concluded that they were acting "normal" only to cover up their paranoia, continued to view them as severely ill, and in fact took their normal behavior to be a clear symptom of illness.

The overriding point is that roles pervade our lives. They are the basis of human organization. They make it possible for us to predict one another's behavior. They provide personal identity. They are crucial to existence. Thus, we have become exceedingly dependent upon them—at the costs of a decline in creativity and mounting stress.

2

Role Stress

THE MEANING OF ROLE STRESS

The difficulties we have in carrying out our social roles can lead to severe psychological, physical, and behavioral disturbances. Only recently has it become clear that role stress is a significant element, often a dominant one, in mental and physical discomfort and illness. While much can be done to alleviate role stress and in fact to turn frustrating role experiences into rewarding ones, in practice this is seldom the case. The reason is that the process by which roles generate stress is not widely understood. Without such understanding, effective remedial action is almost impossible. The central aims of this book are to help provide an understanding of role stress and of ways of effectively coping with it.

Stress, in the general sense, occurs whenever the body is faced with a threat to its integrity. The body goes into a state of alarm. Pituitary and adrenal glands produce hormones that stimulate the body's protective functions. If resolution of the problem soon comes about, the organism returns to its normal state. If the problem is not resolved and persists, the bodily processes continue to signal alarm, the organism experiences exhaustion, and there are debilitating effects. Our psychological and physical health and our participation in everyday life are then affected. Yet, stress is part of life. It acts as a motivating force. Without it, we would quickly wither and die. But too much stress—or too little—will cause psychic and physical pain and will also eventually lead to death.

The basic reason for role stress is this: We have learned through countless episodes of interaction that meeting role expectations leads others to reward us, while failing to do so leads them to punish or otherwise frustrate us. Thus, when we feel we are not able to carry out our roles adequately or that we shall be unable to do so in the future, we are likely to enter a state of physiological alarm. We are often unaware that this is happening and that serves to compound the problem. The more intense the state of alarm and the longer it persists, the more harmful and debilitating its effects are likely to be. The more we are able to cope with the role stress situation, either initially or later, the less harmful its consequences will be.

Role stress can also occur when we carry out our roles adequately, but at too high a cost in psychic or physical energy or the submergence of our needs for self-expression. Again, role stress can result when we feel that role demands on us are excessively low. We may enter a state of alarm because of the absence of challenge. We grow used to the challenge of meeting role expectations and the absence of that challenge can be stressful. Relatedly, loss of roles can lead to stress. The demands of the role are suddenly gone. The familiar behavior patterns can no longer be carried out, although we are geared to do so. The stress of decompression can be severe, in some instances extremely so.

Many of us ordinarily experience minor discomforts because we are unable to cope effectively with role stress. Often we do not see any links between the role problem and its discomforting symptoms. We feel anxious, depressed, have headaches, backaches, feel nauseous, or experience dizziness. Of course, such symptoms are not always due to role stress; yet, many are. If the symptoms appear when role problems mount and disappear some time after those problems subside, then the likelihood of the one causing the other is very great.

Physical and mental problems of a more serious nature are often precipitated by traumatic incidents involving role stress or by prolonged stress due to role problems. Heart attacks, hypertension, peptic ulcers, rheumatoid arthritis, skin disorders, severe depression, hallucinations, paranoid delusions, suicide, and alcoholism are among the many forms of illness and behavior problems that can, in part, be brought about by role stress. Of course, these conditions may be the result of factors other than role stress per se. However, they generally do involve stress factors in one form or another. Recent research has even uncovered the clear possibility of links between role stress and such diseases as cancer, diabetes, and pneumonia.

SOURCES OF ROLE STRESS

There are ten major conditions that commonly lead to role stress. They are discussed at length in Chapter Seven through Chapter Thirteen and so will only be mentioned briefly here. The first three have to do with conflict. *Conflict within a role* occurs when the expectations that others hold for individuals who perform the role are mutually exclusive. If one set of expectations is well met, another cannot be. The role of the industrial foreman is a classic example. He is beholden to management, to his bosses, to labor, and to the men who work under him. They have quite different interests. If he fully meets the expectations of one, it is very difficult to meet those of the others. Thus, he may well have a gnawing sense of failure to perform adequately. He is, as he has often been called, "the man in the middle."

The second source of role stress involves *conflict between two or more of a person's roles*. If one is carried out satisfactorily—that is, according to expectations—it is difficult or impossible to carry out the other adequately. Often this is because one draws time and energy away from the other. The working mother is a good illustration. She may well experience stress. She must slight one role to do the other well, or she persists in carrying out both fully competently at the expense of excessive time and energy, or she compromises on both and feels she does neither well.

Conflict between the role of one person and that of another person is a third source of stress. If one carries out a role adequately, the other is blocked from doing so. They may be at loggerheads with each other, as in a confrontation between police chiefs and protest group leaders.

Highly competitive roles in business are of this type. The more the performer of one does well, the more the performer of the other does poorly. In these three forms of role conflict, there is a "damned if you do and damned if you don't" quality. The individual is likely to feel in a double bind; whichever direction he or she takes is likely to mean that a role is inadequately performed and hence stress tends to result.

The fourth source of stress is sheer *overdemand* in a role. Leaving conflict aside, the role simply demands more in time, energy, ability, or emotional control than the person is able to provide. Experience and training are likely to play a part in whether or not stress occurs, of course. The air controller's role, to be discussed later, is an excellent example. The work is overdemanding in terms of concentration and emotional stamina. In some respects the air controller has little actual control over the situation, but much responsibility. Study after study shows that the resultant stress takes its toll.

Fifth, *undemanding* roles can be as stressful as overdemanding roles. Undemanding roles often require only a simple routine in order to perform them adequately. They are boring. Lack of challenge can be as stressful as excessive challenge. We are trained to strive to meet role demands and when we do not we are likely to feel uneasiness and stress. Work on the assembly line is notoriously debilitating in this way.

The *restrictive* nature of roles is a sixth source of stress. The more roles curb our natural inclinations to express ourselves, to try out new solutions to problems, and to be creative and innovative, the more they lead to stress. Exploratory, problem-solving behavior is the way humans and animals have for millions of years attempted to cope with their environment, to insure their existences. When that behavior is blocked, stress results. Many aforementioned bureaucratic roles in government and industry often do just that. They often demand a set routine, regardless of individual differences and needs. Frequently, they combine underdemand with narrow restrictiveness and so are doubly stressful.

Seventh, the *taking on of new roles* is stressful for most individuals. This may well be so even in the case of highly desirable roles. The uncertainty as to whether one can perform adequately causes stress. Alternately, *ceasing to play roles* is an eighth reason for stress. The marital role, lost through the death of a spouse, and the parental role, lost through the death of a child, are among the most stressful of experiences. The person is sorely missed, but so is the role. The sudden decompression of retirement from the job is a highly stressful experience for many. Even the loss of roles that one is glad to be rid of can be stressful. Behavior patterns one carries out for years are no longer appropriate and must be changed. There is likely to be, at least temporarily, a gnawing vacuum.

Ninth and tenth, role *rejection* and *encroachment* are two further sources of stress. Either fear that one will be rejected in a role or outright rejection is likely to have stressful consequences. Naturally, this may be involved in taking on a new role. It can also happen in a role one has held for some time, as when one's spouse suddenly seeks divorce or when one is fired from a job. Encroachment refers to the attempts, or what we believe to be the attempts, of others to take over part or all of one or more of our roles. Our roles become part of us. They are possessions, social property, and territories of the psyche. Attempts by others to pre-empt us in them cause stress, anguish, and anger.

INDIVIDUAL DIFFERENCES IN EXPERIENCING ROLE STRESS

We all experience these ten forms of role stress many times in our lives. Often we experience several simultaneously. This may occur in various of our roles as when, say, there is severe conflict between two of our roles, we lose a third role, and we are rejected in our attempts to take on another. Alternately, several of these forms of stress can be involved in carrying out a single role. For example, one person's work role may be conflicted and overdemanding, while another's work role may be undemanding and restrictive; in both cases other persons may be encroaching on the role.

When severe difficulties arise in two or more roles simultaneously or in close succession, stress is apt to mount rapidly. Thus, the person who—in a short space of time—is involved in divorce proceedings, moves to a new city (giving up past community roles and taking on new ones), and takes a job there where demands are high and conflicted, is likely to experience a severe stress overload.

In many instances, it is not any one of a person's roles that in itself causes stress. Rather, stress may result from the relationship among several of one's roles. A common example is the person who finds marital, parental, and work roles enjoyable and rewarding when considered one by one. Yet, conflict between work and familial roles may generate much stress. Again, a person's array of roles may be such that each is at least moderately rewarding, yet the overall effect is simply one of too many demands on time and energy.

Individuals vary considerably in how they experience and tolerate role stress. Conditions that bring about harmful stress for one may not cause stress at all for another. Also, stress may occur before, during, or after the actual role situation. If we fear beforehand that we will be unable to meet role expectations and will be punished for failing to do so, then we will experience stress. We may also experience anticipatory stress if we fear that we will lose a role. We may fear that we will lose a role that in fact we do not later lose and experience stress because of that. On the other hand, we may be oblivious to impending role problems and so not feel stress until the time actually arrives. The mentally ill person may not realize that he or she is expected to behave in certain ways in the role of mental patient, yet will later suffer stress in the strait jacket.

When we experience stress in the actual role situation, it is likely to be because we feel we are not measuring up to expectations and will later be punished, or because we are at this point, in fact, actually being punished for our role behavior. We may experience stress after the situation has occurred either because we are being punished or because we also failed to perform adequately and will be punished for that. Also, as noted previously, when a role has been lost we are likely to experience stress because of the behavioral change; we are no longer able to carry out certain behaviors as we once routinely did. The "what you don't know won't hurt you" axiom holds, then, in regard to role stress based on fear of the future, but it does not necessarily hold in or after the situation. For even if one is oblivious to the nature of what has been transpiring, one may later be punished and experience stress.

How we perceive and interpret situations is one important element in role stress. How others react to us is another. A third critical factor is the nature of the resources we have available either to carry out roles satisfactorily and to avoid losing roles, or to cope with the role stress once it has begun to occur. If we feel we have the resources to meet the expectations of a role or to handle the demands of role change and loss, then we are less likely to experience anticipatory role stress. If we actually do possess the resources, we are likely actually to carry out a role satisfactorily or to cope effectively with the loss of a role and so avoid severe stress. If we find ourselves in a stressful role situation, we are best able to terminate the stress if we have access to useful resources. The longer stress persists, the more debilitating it becomes.

Resources take many forms: cultural, social, physiological, and psychological. Whether we have been able to learn the culturally approved, "tried-and-true" ways for coping with stress can make a great difference. This may depend on formal education and training or informal exposure to cultural patterns. Whether we have the social support of family, friends, experts, and so on can be critical. Whether we have the requisite physical strength, stamina, and prowess may be important. Whether, from a psychological standpoint, we have the requisite intelligence, emotional stamina, abilities, and learned behavior patterns can make an enormous difference on the outcome. So can such resources as power, prestige, money, and influence. Things that are positive resources under many conditions may, however, be liabilities in certain role situations. High intelligence may be a detriment in attempting to cope with an unchallenging role that one cannot change. Money occasionally makes it more difficult to carry out roles effectively—especially sudden money. (Sweepstakes winners frequently become overstressed because of the role changes and resent what their luck brings in its wake.)

Finally, some of our roles may be resources for carrying out other roles effectively and for avoiding or coping with stress. A politician may find that his roles as a "family man," a husband, a father of six, and a churchgoing member of a dominant religion may be assets in a variety of ways. A lawyer may be able to cope better with, say, his or her own divorce than one who is not a lawyer. Conversely, roles can, of course, be detrimental to carrying out other roles. The most common illustrations have to do with sex and work roles. We all realize that the female role makes it more difficult for women to gain entrance to and to carry out many work roles. In a much more limited way, this is true of the male role. In such occupations as nurse or kindergarten teacher, the male role can be a burdensome factor.

In sum, whether stress occurs and persists depends on the actual nature of the role situations in which we take part or are stopped from taking part; on our perceptions and interpretations of these situations before, during, and after participation; and on our resources for coping with role problems initially and also with stress once it begins to mount. There is another factor that is equally or more important: our ability to innovate new and effective solutions to role problems. It is this ability, so often absent in stressful situations, that needs to be nurtured, cultivated, and enhanced. That is a theme that recurs throughout this book.

STYLES OF ROLE PERFORMANCE

Depending on past experience and individual attitudes and resources, individuals develop styles of role playing. Style is the imprint that people put on their patterns of behavior. A person may have one style for a particular role and a different style for another (the milktoast at work who is the tyrant at home). Or the same style may cut across the person's various roles. Again, styles are not necessarily unique to given individuals. A group may share a style, as may the members of a whole society. The Ivy Leaguer or the Southern "good old boy" denotes group styles. At the societal level, Europeans often remark on the frank openness of people in or from the United States. We see the Japanese as having an exceedingly polite yet goal-oriented style.

The range of styles is very great. Some of us are aggressive in carrying out one or all of our roles. Some are meek. Some are methodical, others slapdash. Some exude confidence, while others continually display indecisiveness. There are the serious and the humorous, the attentive and the oblivious. There are the deft and the inept, the optimistic and the pessimistic, the emotional and the stoical. The list is very long.

The important point in relation to role stress is that some styles are conducive to satisfactory performance in certain roles and others are not. The indecisive military leader is almost nonexistent and the political leader with an indecisive style is a rarity indeed. Physicians with a meek or seemingly inept style soon turn to psychiatry, research, or preventive medicine. A humorous style can be of great benefit in some roles but it is death to the undertaker. The "clinging-vine" style is hardly an asset to the woman striving to rise in the executive ranks of business. The meek and hesitant television newscaster is indeed difficult to find.

Some of us can switch styles rather readily, as our roles demand.

(Those who do so too readily are likely to become labeled as insincere.) Others switch styles but seem to have a compulsive tendency to match the wrong style to the particular role: boisterousness in church, overly aggressive and assertive behavior with the boss, meek and indecisive behavior with those one supervises. Still others have mainly one style regardless of the role being performed: the plodder, the irreverent, the intellectual.

A style that is seen as unsuitable for a particular role causes consternation in others. It affects, negatively, the evaluation of one's performance, of whether one is meeting expectations. It can cause one to be blocked from assuming a role, to be rejected in a role, or to be forced out of a role. Thus, the "wrong" style can be a definite source of stress, while the "right" style can lessen stress—sometimes greatly.

ROLE STRESS AS SOCIAL CONTROL

If role stress is so debilitating to so many, if it leads to severe behavioral problems as well as to harmful physical and psychological disorders, then why is it so pervasive? Because of social control. Societies use role stress to induce people to conform, to make them predictable, and to get them to produce work. We use role stress as punishment or threat in our attempts to have others act as we want them to act.

We threaten to make it harder for people who do not do our bidding to carry out their roles. We exhort our children to conform or they will have role difficulties later ("You'll be called a sissy."). We threaten the most wayward with the loss of role through imprisonment or mental hospitalization. We fine or demote those whose work does not measure up. We divorce those whose marital behavior we consider intolerable. We encroach on the roles of our competitors.

We give generous monetary and prestigious rewards for the successful carrying out of especially stressful roles. High pressure jobs and high rewards are usually closely connected. Leadership roles in political and economic affairs are good examples. On the other hand, we withhold rewards for the mundane jobs and that too leads to stress. Laborers experience much stress, as we shall see, often more because of the lack of prestige, esteem, and money attached to the work than because of the work itself. The lack of prestige and money means less resources to cope with stress.

We try to discredit the role playing of our enemies. Rumors are floated that a man is a secret homosexual. The small role-playing inadequacies of a fellow worker are repeatedly exaggerated to others. Role traps are set for opponents to fall into in political campaigns. At the same time we try to enhance the role-playing abilities of our allies and friends, and often of ourselves as well.

Much of life is a series of encounters in which individuals facilitate or block one another's role playing. Also, much of life is a struggle to cope with role problems, even apart from whether others try to help or hinder us. Coping with role stress requires skill, perseverance, and often an innovative stance as well.

3

Responses to Role Stress

Roles demand much conformity and so tend to preclude innovative and creative responses to problems that arise from them. This is a major reason why role stress often goes unresolved. The very conformity that is the hallmark of successful role playing works against devising innovative solutions to role problems once they arise.

We commonly use one or more of six broad ways of responding to role stress, most of which are seldom very effective. They may work well in some instances but they often worsen the problem and increase stress. These are aggression toward others, self-destructive behavior, distortion of reality (including mental illness), physical or psychological withdrawal, compulsive conformity, and risk taking. A seventh response, innovation—although less often used—is more likely to be effective. If these responses are insufficiently effective in coping with role stress, and if stress persists at a significant level, then physical illness becomes a further form of response.

AGGRESSION TOWARD OTHERS

Everyone knows that a common response to human problems is to attack someone else, either the person believed to be the cause of the problem or an innocent bystander. This is especially true where role problems are concerned. We are likely to have little understanding of what is causing the problem. We invent a reason—that is, the behavior of one or more other persons. We vent our anger over our predicament on them. We blame and berate them, argue with them, and sometimes physically attack them.

The stereotype of the husband-father who blames his work role problems on his wife and his children has its roots in reality. So does that of the boss who takes his family role problems out on his workers. This displacement of aggression to the wrong source almost always has negative consequences. A son or daughter becomes rebellious and turns to delinquency. A wife sues for divorce. Workers engage in sabotage. A good deal of the contention between people is essentially of this type: One aggresses against the other for the wrong reasons and the other retaliates. Again, each may be displacing aggression over role problems to the other.

A person may blame and aggress against another simply because the other is carrying out a role adequately. We grow angry with the police officer for arresting us, although we were far exceeding the speed limit. We damn the boss who signs our retirement papers, although he may have little choice if he is to continue in his job. This form of aggression obviously does not get at the root of the matter and only makes enemies.

However, if other persons are making unreasonable demands—demands above and beyond role demands—then some clear indication to them that that will not be tolerated may have its advantages. We vent our feelings and they may cease their demands. If you are a waiter or waitress, it does no good to become angry with customers or kitchen workers because of conflicting demands. On the other hand, if the chef insists that the waiter or waitress convince the customer that accidentally overseasoned food contains no seasoning, then that is an unreasonable and idiosyncratic demand.

The basic necessity is to distinguish between difficult people and difficult role conditions. If our difficulties arise from a role problem, then some change in our roles is required. If the problem is actually rooted in another person, then one of two broad remedies is indicated: Induce the person to change or avoid that person.

Any response may be used in an attempt to cope with any type of role problem. However, certain responses are more likely to be used in relation to some role problems than others. Aggression is a common response to role conflict and overdemand. It may also often be used in instances of role restriction, rejection or encroachment, and occasionally in taking on new roles. Aggression is less likely to be the response when roles are undemanding or in the case of role loss. The more the person construes, however erroneously, that a role problem is due to other specific persons, the greater the probability of an aggressive response. The lack of challenge and the boredom that comes from undemanding roles are seldom seen as being due to the negative actions of others. While loss of a role may very well be attributed to another person, often it is seen as due to impersonal social forces (mandatory retirement) or to "natural" causes (death of a loved one due to an accident) or to some liability of oneself.

Aggression toward others ranges from that which is directly physical to the most subtle psychological attack. Killing, assaulting, threatening with physical harm, arguing, attacking the credibility, the social standing, and the role-playing ability of others, and psychologically rejecting children—these are all forms of aggression. Much of this aggression occurs within the family or between friends. The mass media play up the attack in the night of the stranger upon the innocent victim. We are intrigued by that. However, most aggression occurs between people who know each other well: husbands and wives assaulting each other, child abuse (which includes psychological as well as physical attacks on children, often by their parents), serious quarrels between lovers, workers seeking to attack each other through trying either to make each other's role playing on the job more difficult or to diminish the other's role responsibilities and reputation for adequate role playing.

SELF-DESTRUCTIVE BEHAVIOR

Behavior that is destructive to the self is also a common response to stress. Here individuals may inwardly castigate or blame themselves for real or supposed shortcomings. Of course, realistic self-evaluation can be extremely constructive and healthy. However, self-blame that goes beyond that can only be demoralizing and self-defeating in the long run. At its most extreme, self-destructive behavior—that is, aggression against the self—takes the form of attempted or actual suicide. Lesser forms of self-destructive behavior are often excesses of one kind or another: overworking; excessive eating, smoking, drinking, or use of other drugs; and even overexercising. These behaviors provide a target, ourselves, for the aggression we feel in the face of stress. At the same time, they reduce anxiety in the short run. Overwork is an escape. The excessive intake of smoke, alcohol, or food has a calming effect.

We tend to engage in self-blame and to become aggressive toward ourselves when we do not perceive others as being at fault. Certain types of role loss are especially likely to lead to this form of response. When we lose a job through retirement, a spouse through death, or our children because they grow up and move away, there is usually no one to blame. We tend to be overcome by a sense of helplessness. A part of us is gone. The self may become a residual target for the suppressed anger we feel. Blaming the self is doing *something*, taking some action.

Similarly, when roles are undemanding we are likely to experience a nameless frustration over the absence of challenge. On the surface, things are not so terrible. A job is a job, one gets paid—even if one's abilities go unused—and so on. But the boredom eats away at one. No one is making unreasonable demands, so no one else is likely to be blamed. Again, the self may become the target of the anger that our frustration generates.

It may seem that to blame the self for role problems such as these borders on the irrational. The fact remains: Self-aggression in the face of role stress is fairly common and tends to be a displacement to ourselves of our anger over those unseen forces that seem to work against us. In regard to the most extreme form of self-destructive behavior, suicide, there are these well-established research findings: Persons who lost one or both parents in childhood through divorce, desertion, or death are twice as likely later to commit suicide than persons who did not suffer such losses; suicide rates are also twice as high for persons who in adulthood have lost through death spouses, parents, children, or close friends; and the risk of suicide is still greater among those who lost family and friendship roles in both childhood and adulthood.

The suicide rate is in part a very good measure of the role stress level of a population. A county, a region, a state of the United States, an occupational category, a marital category (single, married, widowed, divorced), a social class group—these are all population entities whose stress levels can be gauged to some extent by their suicide rates.

DISTORTION

We unconsciously distort our perceptions of our role problems in an attempt to lessen stress. We close our eyes to the real situation. We firmly believe that we are doing a good job when all objective indicators point the other way. We sometimes refuse to recognize role loss. Again, we may imagine that some actually irrelevant person or force is the cause of our difficulties.

The human capacity for distortion and self-deception is large. This is not entirely a bad thing. Some softening of the harsher realities of life can be exceedingly helpful in getting through role crises. Too much facing of "the truth" head on can be excessively debilitating. Distortion is a psychological defense with certain definite advantages.

Yet, in its more extreme forms, distortion means the loss of being in touch with reality. The person perceives things less painfully than he or she otherwise would through mistaken and false—that is, paranoid—beliefs. In some instances, the development of multiple personalities allows the individual to cope selectively with otherwise insurmountable problems. It is by no means uncommon for mental illness to develop as an adaptation to severe persistent role problems. The person then sees life in a way fundamentally different from others. The role-playing ability of the individual tends to break down because of the persistent gulf between him or her and others over the nature of role demands. Others then assign to the person the mentally ill role. This is a very real role, especially in mental hospitals. The role expectations of others, that the individual *act* mentally ill, reinforces and perpetuates the symptoms of mental illness.

Extreme distortion is not especially connected to any particular form of role stress. Rather, it tends to come into play when the individual is exposed to severe role stress in *any* form for an extended period and for one reason or another cannot cope with it by other means.

Interestingly, there appears to be, to some extent, an inverse relationship between psychosis—mainly schizophrenia—and physical illness. Those persons who are psychotic and distort reality to a large degree have distinctly less physical illness than their "normal" counterparts.

WITHDRAWAL

In one way or another, we may remove ourselves from the stressful role situation. We may, in extreme cases, go beyond distortion and become psychologically oblivious to our plight. Catatonic schizophrenia is an extreme illustration: The person is immobilized for hours at a time and sensory perception is largely blocked off. The use of drugs, such as alcohol—apart from being self-destructive—may accomplish somewhat the same end.

Again, a person may literally leave the stressful role situation temporarily or permanently. The judicious use of physical escape can be a beneficial response. "Sticking to one's guns, come hell or high water" may, in some instances, lead to physical or psychological breakdown. A strategically timed vacation to see one through a role crisis may be sensible. Missing work for a day or two because of a stress overload may be adaptive indeed. The problem, of course, is that escape can readily become an abortive crutch. A reputation for being absent when things get tough can obviously be damaging to one also, especially in certain work situations, and can lead to further role stress. Moreover, if escape means leaving others in the lurch, role problems for them and additional problems for oneself are likely to ensue.

As with distortion, withdrawal may be used as a response to any form of role stress. However, there is some tendency for physical flight to be associated with role conflict, overdemand, and rejection. If there seems no way to resolve conflict or reduce demands, fleeing the situation may be the most immediate remedy. Also, the humiliation of rejection sometimes drives individuals to flee. Psychological withdrawal is more common in instances of underdemand, restrictive roles, and role loss. Either physical or psychological withdrawal may be a response to encroachment on one's roles, especially if the person doing the encroaching is powerful. More often, however, the response to encroachment is the territorial response of animals, "stand and fight."

COMPULSIVE CONFORMITY

This is in some respects quite the opposite of flight. The person continues in the role, performing in the same way, regardless of the consequences. Stress can lead to rigidity and compulsive repetition of behavior, sometimes called ritualizing. The person does what is familiar and hopes that somehow the problem will pass. It seldom does. Some illustrations of this are: a person in role conflict, such as a foreman, who keeps attempting to conform to and to fulfill contradictory demands, although to do so has become clearly impossible; the worker, whose efficiency report points to a tendency to be overly concerned with irrelevant details, who becomes even more concerned with those same details; the retired person who keeps going around to the former place of work.

Overconformity flourishes in the bureaucratic setting. Stress results from role expectations that are restrictive and are often undemanding as well. The individual responds with even greater conformity than that demanded by expectations. This is the behavior of the bureaucrat in the large hospital who insists upon the correct filling out of complicated patient admission forms; meanwhile the would-be patient dies. This is the behavior of the librarian who attempts to keep each book in its proper place on the shelves, although that means denying books to the public. Mixed with a liberal dose of aggression, it is the behavior of the marine drill sergeant who runs his men in the broiling sun all day, then orders them into the swamp where seven out of twenty die.

Overconformity is sometimes referred to sociologically as ritualism. The individual is preoccupied with means and loses sight of the ends to which the means lead. He or she ritualistically performs the means, goes beyond the norms, and in so doing tends to abort the ends the means are meant to accomplish. Such compulsive behavior may have the short-run effect of reducing anxiety through reiteration of the familiar. Clearly, however, its long-run consequences can be disastrous because stress is likely to continue unabated. This is especially so outside of bureaucratic structures congenial to ritualism.

RISK-TAKING

Every time you drive or walk along a road, there is some risk of being injured or killed. Risk is part and parcel of life. We turn to it as a way of attempting to resolve role problems mainly for two reasons. First of all, our resources for coping with stress may be meager and we may see no reasonable alternative. Thus, the failing student cheats on examinations in an effort to graduate. The politician stakes all on one speech in which he hopes to turn the tide of public criticism of him. The man or woman whose business is failing enters into a highly risky financial deal or takes a plunge in the stock market in a do-or-die effort to put himself or herself on sound fiscal ground.

The second major reason why people turn to risk taking is as an antedote to the depression that often accompanies role loss or the boredom of undemanding roles. Risk taking roils the stagnant waters of apathy and energizes the system, at least for the moment. Gambling, high-speed driving, and even certain forms of crime are used to alleviate depression and boredom. Regarding the last, some middle class housewives with little to do turn to shoplifting as a form of excitement. Notice that roles themselves may be risked. The housewife risks her middle class standing through larceny. The person in business may repeatedly risk financial ruin. Role risk is also an integral ingredient of politics.

Much more than is generally realized, accidents are the outcome of unconsciously motivated risk taking. The person is under role stress often because of loss. He or she is desperately seeking a solution, a way out. None presents itself. Below the level of conscious awareness, the individual's organism moves itself into a risk position—on the highway, on the job, on the stock market. That process in itself is rewarding. It leads to changes in the bodily processes—to the release of adrenaline, for example. It dispels a sense of helplessness and relieves depression. It provides a quick fix. Then it can become an end in itself. Moreover, self-destruction impulses can be satisfied if the risk outcome is negative. Risking anything time and again inevitably means disaster eventually.

Individuals favor one or another of these six forms of response depending on past experience and learning. And, as has been indicated, some of the responses are more likely to be used when certain role problems confront us than when others do. There is no overall rule, however. Any one of these responses may be employed when a person faces role stress from any of the sources previously outlined. Frequently, of course, a person attempts to cope with role stress by using several of these responses simultaneously.

PHYSICAL ILLNESS

Two other major forms of response to role stress are innovation and physical illness. If the individual cannot cope effectively with role stress through the use of the six responses discussed above, and is also unable to cope innovatively with that stress, then physical illness may result. Certain sudden and very traumatic role changes—for example, the fact or threat of severe role loss—may also trigger physical illness.

As noted in Chapter Two, role stress can lead not only to headaches, backaches, nausea, dizziness, and other relatively minor physical symptoms; a wide variety of serious illnesses have been associated with one or another form of role stress. Some serious illnesses that can be linked to role stress are heart disease, hypertension, peptic ulcers, colitis, rheumatoid arthritis, and numerous skin disorders. In addition, certain forms of cancer and leukemia, diabetes, and pneumonia have been pointed to in recent research as role stress related. Obviously, these illnesses may result from many factors other than role stress. The important point here is that stress due to role and other social problems can be and often is a significant contributory factor.

The research evidence that points to role stress as a source of illness and disease, some of which is summarized in the succeeding chapters, is very strong. Why, then, has so little attention been given to it? It flies in the face of established medical knowledge. It is not understood by most physicians. It is, for the most part, not treatable by usual medical methods. Changes in the social environment and the behavior of the individual are required, rather than changes in the organism per se. The fact remains—people who are unable to cope effectively with role stress that is either severe and persistent or exceedingly traumatic during a given short period succumb to disease in far greater numbers than other persons of their age who are not under stress.

Hans Selye, the great pioneer in stress research, pointed out decades ago that the initial response of the organism to stress is alarm. This is followed by resistance, the body's marshaling of its defenses. If resistance is insufficient and stress continues, the defense system winds down and exhaustion results. The stage is set for the onset of disease. Stewart Wolf has characterized the individual's psychosomatic response to socially induced stress as the "as if" response. The individual's body is reacting as if it were confronted with a physical assault on it. The organism with coronary heart disease is reacting as if enormous effort to ward off danger were perpetually required. The hypertensive person's organism is reacting as if it were about to suffer the loss of blood due to wounding. The organism with diabetes is responding as if it were faced with starvation.

An important side effect of physical illness, of course, is that it may be sufficiently incapacitating to cause the person to be removed from the sources of role stress. Physical illness is generally a socially acceptable basis for setting aside many role responsibilities. Taking on the role of the sick person automatically precludes or suspends the carrying out of various other roles.

COPING INNOVATIVELY

Think of the terrible pressures that many feel to perform adequately as a male or a female, as a sexual partner, as a parent, as a student, or as a worker striving after material proof of success. The prevailing role expectations are routinely accepted as if they constituted an intrinsic, immutable system of values. Little thought is given to the fact that they are simply the performance standards of the day, the yardsticks of conformity. Hardly anyone asks the fundamental question of whether prevailing role expectations are harmful or beneficial to society and to the individual. Still fewer of us explore how roles might be changed or modified to make life more enjoyable. Yet we have the power to change roles, not only to shift from one role to another, but to change roles we or others will continue to carry out. The first step is to understand the nature of roles, how they operate, and how they cause stress. The next step is to bring about role change.

The key to coping effectively with role stress is innovation. Innovation is the process of putting two or more ideas or things together in a new way so that a problem is solved. It is as useful in coping with role stress as it is in inventing a much needed machine, in constructing a better theory of the universe, or in "finding a better way to build a mousetrap" in everyday life.

We are all basically innovative. Innovation is the stuff of survival. It is what has made humans an exceedingly durable species. All children are innovative and creative until it is stamped out of them by the pressures to conform to social roles. Roles—with few exceptions, then—suppress innovation. They also generate much stress, and stress in itself makes us rigid—a further enemy of innovation. Hence, we are faced with the triple negative of role stress, rigidity, and little innovative experience in how to cope with stress.

Yet finding effective solutions to role problems is essentially the same as finding solutions to problems of other kinds. One must first understand the cause of the difficulty, innovate and weigh alternative solutions, consider workable resources, devise a plan of action, try out that plan, and modify it. This requires the knowledge of roles, the ability to think things out, flexibility, and an experimental approach.

The first necessary step, then, is to determine if a role stress problem exists. One or more of a variety of symptoms will be present: anxiety, depression, anger, compulsions, undue risk taking, erratic behavior, excessive drinking of alcohol or use of other drugs, and such psychosomatic symptoms as headaches, abdominal pain, backaches, nausea, blurred vision, heart palpitation, and general weakness. As emphasized earlier, these may be due to some underlying conventional medical problem rather than to role stress. If they are not, then they are very likely signals that role stress is either rising or persisting at harmful levels.

The second step is to understand the role stress problem. Is the problem one of conflict within a role or between roles? Is it one of overdemand, underdemand, or restrictiveness? Or is it one of role change: taking on a new role, loss of a role, rejection in a role, or encroachment by another on a role? Any combination of these may be generating stress. Which of the person's roles are centrally involved? Are other people and their roles necessarily affected?

Once the source of role stress is determined, the necessity is to innovate a number of possible solutions. This requires sitting back, gaining some psychological distance from one's own roles, attempting to look at the problem from various perspectives, not being afraid to consider seemingly outlandish strategies, and not being afraid to be creative. Given that, do one's available resources allow a given approach to be taken? If so, what appear to be the gains and losses of that approach? Is it likely to lead to other role problems that may cause as much or more stress as the present ones? Put simply, will a given approach do the job? And finally, how do we determine when a role problem has been solved? These are matters addressed in the final chapters of this book.

4

Prestige and
Occupational Roles

Study after study of physical and mental health, illness, and behavior problems points to role stress as a major source of difficulty. Among the best indicators of stress are when and how people die. Alexander Leaf, a physician at Harvard, analyzed the reasons for longevity among three especially long-lived peoples: those of Abkahazia in the Caucasus Mountains of Southern Russia; those of Hunza, a remote area of Pakistan; and those of Vilcahambra in the Andes Mountains of Ecuador. Many of those groups are still vigorous at ages over one hundred. Leaf's conclusion: In addition to taking a positive view of the world, exercising through work, and other factors, those who live very long lives hold relatively prestigious and *needed* roles. "People who no longer have a necessary role to play in the social and economic life of their society generally deteriorate rapidly."

James Lynch, a researcher on heart disease, concluded in his book, *The Broken Heart*, that a major factor in heart disorders and deaths due to heart disease is loneliness. And what so often constitutes this loneliness? Failure to take on roles that place one in ongoing intimate relationships with others. Equally important is the loss of such roles. A lack of the roles that contribute to closeness with others, especially the absence of the marital role of husband or wife, leads all too often to a "broken heart."

Meyer Friedman and Ray H. Rosenman, the cardiologists who wrote *Type A Behavior and Your Heart*, found that a major cause of heart attacks and death was a personality that was incessantly involved in aggressive competition and hostile struggle with others and one that was obsessed with compressing that activity into shorter and shorter time periods. Why are the role relationships of these Type A individuals, usually men? They are often locked in role conflict with others and are striving mightily to meet excessive role demands. And they have substituted ritualistic struggle for innovative response.

PRESTIGE ROLES

One of the consistent findings in research on stress is that the lower the prestige roles of individuals the more stress they experience, the less able are they to cope with it, and the more debilitating its outcome. While there are definite exceptions to this, as a broad generalization it is very sound. The more prestigious, influential, and powerful persons are often able to avoid restrictive roles that the less prestigious cannot. They have the resources to fend off encroachment on their roles and potential role rejection and loss more effectively than those of low prestige. When they do lose roles, they have more resources for coping with loss. Undemanding roles can be a serious problem for those of high prestige as it can be for low prestige persons, but for different reasons. The latter are often relegated to work roles that demand little. The very prestigious and wealthy sometimes lack incentive to take on demanding roles. However, those of considerable but not the greatest prestige frequently do hold work roles that are in fact demanding and conflicted. But they are likely to possess the intellectual and other skills to cope with demands and also to cope with stress once it occurs. One not unimportant point is that when stress begins to mount the well-to-do can take time off, take a vacation, or go on a trip much more readily than the less well-to-do. They also have far more access to medical and psychological services. As a result, rates of mental illness, physical illness, and death are far greater for those in the lower than the upper classes.

Occupation is often used as a good measure of prestige or social class standing. As in Table 4.1, occupations are usually classified into nine prestige groups, with the professions ranking the highest and laboring jobs the lowest. Table 4.1 gives standard mortality ratios for working men in the United States aged 20 to 64. The standard mortality ratio (SMR) for male workers in all occupations is 100. An SMR of 200 would mean that in that group the likelihood of death within a specified period is twice the average for all males aged 20 to 64. An SMR of 50 would mean the likelihood of death in a given period is half the average. Comparing a group with an SMR of 50 with one with an SMR of 200, one can say that those persons in the latter group are four times more likely to die in a specified period than those in the former group.

Table 4.1   Standard Mortality Ratios by Major Occupational Groups, Men Aged 20 to 64, United States, 1950

		ALL CAUSES	HEART DISEASE [a]
	Professional & Technical	88	102
High prestige	Managers, Officials, Proprietors	89	100
	Clerical	84	95
	Sales	96	110
	Craftsmen, Foremen	99	100
	Operatives	96	92
Low prestige	Service Workers [b]	118	115
	Laborers, Except Farm & Mine	163	141
	Farm Laborers	96	89
	All Occupations	100	100

SOURCE: Lillian Guralnick, *Mortality by Occupation and Cause of Death among Men 20 to 64 Years of Age: United States, 1950*, Washington, D.C.: U.S. Department of Health, Education and Welfare, Vital Statistics–Special Reports, vol. 53, no. 3, Sept. 1963.

[a] Cardiovascular-renal diseases.

[b] Excludes private household workers who had SMR of 54 for all causes of death.

Table 4.1 gives SMRs for all causes of death combined and for heart disease, a distinctly stress-related cause of death. Service workers and laborers are much more likely to die within a given period than those in higher prestige categories. This is true for all causes of death and for heart disease. (Farm laborers are the exception; farm life is not stressful.)

In fact, the SMR of 163 for laborers for all causes of death is about *twice* that of professionals, technicals, managers, officials, proprietors, and clericals.

The level of educational attainment is another excellent measure of prestige standing and has the benefit of being applicable to everyone, not just to those in the work force. Table 4.2 shows that SMRs for all causes of death combined go down dramatically for both white men and women as the level of education increases. Males with four or less years of school have an SMR of 115 while those who are college graduates have an SMR of 70. The former are 1.6 times more likely to die within a specified period than the latter. The differences are even greater for women. For those with four or less years of schooling the SMR is 160; for college graduates it is 78. The uneducated females are twice as likely to die within a specified period as the highly educated. (The fact that college educated males have a lower SMR, 70, than college educated females, 78, is not in itself significant. SMRs can be compared only within the male or female group, not between the two. Differences by sex are discussed shortly.)

Table 4.2 Standard Mortality Ratios by Years of School Completed, White Men and Women Aged 25 to 64, United States, 1950–1960

YEARS OF SCHOOL COMPLETED	ADULT MALES 25 TO 64 SMR ALL CAUSES	ADULT WOMEN 25 TO 64 SMR ALL CAUSES
0–4	115	160
5–7	114	118
8	107	108
9–11	105	91
12	91	87
13–15	85	82
16 or more	70	78
All	100	100

SOURCE: Evelyn M. Kitagawa and Philip M. Hauser, *Differential Mortality in the United States: A Study in Socioeconomic Epidemiology*, Cambridge, Mass.: Harvard University Press, 1973, p. 12.

The same general patterns hold when blacks in the United States are compared with whites. Those of lower prestige as a race, the blacks, have higher death rates for most causes of death. This is especially so for death due to hypertension, decidedly a stress-related disease. Average length of life also varies greatly for the two races. For example, whites born in the United States in 1975 will live on the average five and one-half years longer than non-whites (over nine-tenths of whom are black), 73.2 years to 67.9 years. As a race, blacks hold stressful jobs or none at all. They have less education than whites, more disorganized and stressful family relationships, less money, less medical facilities, and less resources to cope with stress.

OCCUPATIONAL ROLES

Work roles vary tremendously in the extent to which they are stressful. Some are exceedingly so, others almost not at all. While jobs of low prestige are likely to be more stressful than those of high, there are important exceptions. Farm laborers were mentioned as exceptions in the low prestige category. Air controllers, in the moderately high prestige range, are under severe stress. So are physicians, a very high prestige category. Even though they have many resources to cope with stress, physicians have somewhat high rates of heart disease, alcoholism, drug addiction, and suicide. The time and energy demands of their work, living with illness and death, and conflict with family roles outweigh, to some extent, their abilities to cope effectively with stress.

Of course, certain work roles are just plain dangerous. Those in construction work because of accidents and those in asbestos factories because of lung cancer are examples. Apart from such obviously dangerous roles, death rates of men in various occupations are good indicators of the stressfulness of work rules. Death rates attributed to cardiovascular-renal disease—that is, heart problems—are especially good barometers of stress.

Table 4.3 gives the standard mortality rates (SMR) for men in the United States in twenty occupations. This table should be interpreted in the same general way as Tables 4.1 and 4.2. If workers in a given occupation have an SMR of 200, that means they are twice as likely to die before age sixty-five as male workers in general. If workers in another occupation have an SMR of fifty, they are only half as likely to die before sixty-five as workers generally.

Table 4.3 Standard Mortality Ratios by Occupation,
Men Aged 20 to 64, United States, 1950–1960

	ALL CAUSES	HEART DISEASE [a]		ALL CAUSES	HEART DISEASE [a]
All Occupations	100	100	Waiters &		
Cooks in			Bartenders	116	105
Restaurants	180	163	Clergymen	109	133
Longshoremen	164	147	Physicians &		
Musicians	162	169	Surgeons	91	111
Taxi Drivers	149	155	Lawyers & Judges	90	106
Tailors	143	150	Dentists	87	101
Police Officers	137	157	Mail Carriers	68	75
Bakers	126	127	Elementary & High		
Machinists	126	138	School Teachers	61	71
Pharmacists	126	140	Natural Scientists	56	64
Real Estate			College Presidents		
Agents	126	146	& Professors	52	65
			Social Scientists	45	62

SOURCE: Lillian Guralnick, *Mortality by Occupation and Cause of Death among Men 20 to 64 Years of Age: United States, 1950*, Washington, D.C.: U.S. Department of Health, Education and Welfare, Vital Statistics–Special Reports, vol. 53, no. 3, Sept. 1963.

[a] Cardiovascular-renal diseases.

Table 4.3 shows that cooks, longshoremen, musicians, and taxi drivers tend to lead highly stressful lives as indicated by SMRs for all causes of death and for heart disease. Social and natural scientists, college presidents and professors, and elementary and high school teachers are at the opposite end of the scale and have low SMRs. Cooks have an SMR for all causes of death of 180, while for social scientists the figure is 45. Thus, male cooks are four times as likely to die before age 65 as male social scientists are. Those who work as cooks, longshoremen, musicians, and taxi drivers have occupations that demand much repetition and hence are boring but also demand much sheer work during some of the day. The scientists and teachers have jobs that require ingenuity and that are a challenge but not to the extent of being burdensome and stressful.

A 1977 study analyzed hospital records and death certificates of both male and female workers in 130 occupations in Tennessee. Using illness and death rates as the major criteria, the twelve most stressful work roles were found to be these:

1. Unskilled Laborer
2. Secretary
3. Assembly Line Inspector
4. Clinical Lab Technician
5. Office Manager
6. Foreman
7. Manager or Administrator
8. Waitress or Waiter
9. Factory Machine Operator
10. Farm Owner
11. Miner
12. House Painter

Two of these work roles, unskilled laborer and factory machine operator, demand very little except routine activity. This is also true of the miner and the house painter. In addition, the miner suffers the stress of dangerous work and the house painter is continually exposed to toxic fumes. Four of the jobs, assembly line inspector, office manager, foreman, and waitress or waiter, make conflicting demands. (In the first three of those the demands of workers and management conflict; in the last one the demands of customers, kitchen help, and management conflict.) The work of the manager or administrator and the farm owner entails much direct responsibility. The remaining two stressful occupations, secretary and clinical lab technician, are stressful because of their marginality. They work as sub-professionals in distinctly professional settings.

The twelve least stressful occupations in the Tennessee study, as indicated by low death and illness rates, were:

1. Clothing Sewer
2. Garment Checker
3. Stock Clerk
4. Skilled Craftsman
5. Maid
6. Farm Laborer
7. Heavy Equipment Operator
8. Freight Handler
9. Child Care Worker
10. Factory Package Wrapper
11. College Professor
12. Personnel Worker

Many of these jobs are not especially demanding and, in fact, involve much routine. However, most allow one to work at one's own pace. This is little conflict. The skilled craftsman, child care worker, college professor, and personnel worker, are in their separate ways demanding but provide a sense of challenge, achievement, and reward. A special quality attaches to operating heavy equipment such as bulldozers; for many men, expressing power through a machine can be a great tension reducer.

In the same study, an analysis was made of the extent to which individuals in different occupations were admitted to mental hospitals for psychiatric disorders of various kinds. Here are the twelve leading occupations, beginning with the one with the highest admission rate:

1. Health Technician
2. Waiter or Waitress
3. Practical Nurse
4. Inspector
5. Musician
6. Public Relations Person
7. Clinical Laboratory Technician
8. Dishwasher
9. Warehouseman
10. Nurse's Aide
11. Laborer
12. Dental Assistant

Five of these, health technician, practical nurse, clinical laboratory technician, nurse's aide, and dental assistant, are related to hospital and health care. Moreover, two other health care occupations, health aide and registered nurse, also rank high on the list but below twelfth place. Hospitals are stressful environments. Working with ill people outside of hospitals is also stress-inducing. Additionally, these workers have considerable responsibility for the welfare of patients but lack the authority to improve conditions. There is always the possibility, of course, that some persons with psychiatric problems gravitate into health occupations so that they will have ready access to professional advice concerning those problems should it be needed.

As is found in most studies of mental illness and sex roles, female workers were admitted to mental hospitals more frequently than male workers. While females comprised 39 percent of the employed population, 53 percent of hospital admissions were females. Males comprised 61 percent of the work force, but they only made up 47 percent of hospital admissions.

Data on the stress factor in the work roles of females have generally not been systematically collected and are still scarce. There are indications, as women move into stressful occupations traditionally filled by men, that their rates of illness will increase and their length of life will decrease. One study found that young women physicians have distinctly higher death rates than women of their age in the general population. This may be due to stress of the occupation per se. It may be due, in part, to the fact that medicine is dominated by males and the female role is alien to that setting.

In any case, female workers are vulnerable to conflict between their sex role and job role when they are employed in male dominated settings. The same is true for males in female dominated work roles—male nurses, for example. Additionally, many females in the labor force experience severe stress due to conflict between their wife-mother and work roles. This is discussed in Chapter Eight.

5

Sex Roles and Marriage

MALE AND FEMALE ROLES

Biology, of course, plays a part in the nature of the male and female roles. Women bear the children and men have greater physical strength. Yet in some societies women do most of the heavy work. The most outstanding female athletes can seldom best the most outstanding male athletes in competition; but those females can easily win over *most* males. There is some evidence that, in general, females may be less aggressive than males. Yet in several societies women kill their own children more often than men do. It is fair to say that while biology may set some limiting conditions on male and female behavior, most of how the two sexes respond to life's problems is determined by the way male and female roles have developed in the given society.

Everyone is aware that the female role in this and many other countries is now changing rapidly. Less well understood is that the male role is changing with about equal rapidity. There are female roles only

46

because there are male roles and vice versa. Without one there could not be the other. We talk more about change in the female role, so we conclude there is more change occurring in it.

The levels of stress brought about by changes in the two roles may vary considerably, however, even though the rates of change are similar. The female role is becoming one that is less characterized by the sometimes boring and restrictive housewife's role and more characterized by conflict between the demands of the home and of the job and other outside activities. The male role shows signs of shifting from one of high competition "in the market place" to one that keeps the man in the home more and that is less demanding.

While many people would vehemently argue otherwise, most of the evidence points to the female role as having been less stressful than the male role in the United States. This does not mean that the woman's role has been one of low stress, only that the man's role has very likely been more so. Change in the two roles may now be redressing this imbalance.

What we are really talking about here are sex roles as they influence individuals' other roles and the stress they encounter. The male role leads men into occupational and other roles that are especially stressful. The female role has traditionally left women unexposed to occupational stress in the usual sense, although the housewife's role has clearly had stresses of its own. In any case, consider some of the evidence as to stress experienced by the two sexes. Longevity and death rates, especially those due to cardiovascular death and to suicide, are good indications of lifelong stress.

Females live longer than males, in part because of lower levels of prolonged role stress. Females born in the United States in 1975 can expect, on the average, to live almost eight years longer than males—77.2 years as compared to 69.4 years. That is, the average life expectancy for females is 11 percent greater than that for males. The death rate for females in the United States is three-fourths that of males. In 1975, out of every 100,000 males, 1,013 died within the year as compared to a figure of 770 for females. At ages 60 to 64, the female death rate was one-half the male rate, 1,227 to 2,523. Of living persons aged 65 and over in 1975, about 60 percent were females.

Males aged twenty-five and over in this country are 1.6 times more likely to die of cardiovascular-renal diseases than females and 1.4 times more likely to die of malignant neoplasms. Males are three times more likely than females to commit suicide and four times more likely to be victims of homicide. However, females attempt suicide unsuccessfully several times more frequently than males.

The emphasis in the male role on assertiveness, aggressiveness, dominance, competitiveness, and the need to maintain a macho image places much stress on the man. This transfers to job and other roles. Studies of heart patients indicate clearly that these aggressive qualities have much to do with coronary artery and heart diseases. The studies of Friedman and Roseman of Types A and B personalities show that Type A men have three times as great a likelihood of coronary heart disease as Type B men. Type A men try hard to be dominant and assertive, while Type B men do not. The same pattern holds among females, but there are far fewer Type A females than males.

On the other hand, women report symptoms of physical and mental illness more than men and use physicians and hospitals more than men. Whether females are more prone to report health problems than males or actually have a higher incidence of these problems is unclear. One fairly certain point is that women suffer more than men from depressive mental disorders. This is probably a result of the restrictive and at times undemanding, and therefore depressive, nature of the housewife role.

At the same time, the female role allows for more expression of emotion than the male role. It is more acceptable for females to cry, complain, and commiserate with each other than it is for males. In a word, females are not *expected* to live up to a macho image, while males are. This may well be an especially significant factor in explaining the lower death rates and longer length of life of females as compared to males.

MARITAL ROLES

Those who are married certainly have role problems, sometimes very severe ones. But the role stress of unmarried persons—single, widowed, or divorced—is usually far greater. The married role is all in all a supportive one; husbands and wives generally help each other more often than not. The single person does not have that support. Divorced and widowed persons have lost it, often traumatically, through the contention that can precede divorce or through the anguish over a loved one's death.

Among persons aged fifteen to sixty-four in the period 1959 to 1961 in the United States, the *death rates per 1,000* population for men and women and white and non-white in the various marital role categories were:

	MARRIED	SINGLE	WIDOWED	DIVORCED	TOTAL
White Males	8.8	15.3	15.5	20.1	9.7
Non-White Males	13.6	22.7	25.8	25.4	15.7
White Females	4.5	6.0	5.9	6.2	4.8
Non-White Females	9.9	14.1	16.4	10.5	11.7

These rates are adjusted to take into account that widowed people tend to be older and single people tend to be younger than married people. For all sex and race groups, the married have distinctly the lowest death rates. The differences are more striking among males than females. For example, the death rate of 20.1 for divorced white males is two and one-half times as great as that of 8.8 for married white males; the death rate of 6.2 for divorced white females is not quite half again as high as that of 4.5 for married white females.

For every marital category, the death rates of non-whites—male and female—are higher than for their white counterparts. Being unmarried and having low prestige (non-white, mainly black) produces especially high death rates, particularly for males. Widowed non-white males have a rate of 25.8, over *five* times the rate of 4.5 for married white females.

Cigarette smoking has been clearly associated with disease and death. Yet, interestingly, much of the association of smoking with high death rates is affected by marital status. Married males aged forty to sixty-nine years who do not smoke have an annual death rate (standardized for age) of 796 per 100,000 while those married males who smoke twenty or more cigarettes a day have a death rate of twice that, 1,560. *Divorced males who do not smoke show a death rate of 1,420, almost as great as married males who do smoke.* Divorced males who do smoke have an especially high death rate, 2,675. The effects of widowhood are much the same. Here are the data:

Age-Standardized Death Rates
per 100,000 Males, Aged 40–69

	NON-SMOKERS	SMOKE 20+ CIGARETTES A DAY
Married	796	1,560
Single	1,074	2,567
Widowed	1,396	2,570
Divorced	1,420	2,675

Death rates due to coronary heart disease and hypertensive disease are good measures of lifelong stress. For persons in the United States aged thirty-five to forty-four years, *death rates per 100,000* population for coronary heart disease were as follows:

	MARRIED	SINGLE	WIDOWED	DIVORCED
White Males	81.1	119.0	149.0	200.0
Non-White Males	77.7	158.5	202.6	188.3
White Females	11.8	24.6	27.6	25.3
Non-White Females	41.4	75.8	100.2	55.8

For all four sex-race groups, rates for single individuals for death from coronary disease distinctly exceed those for married persons; widowed and divorced persons' rates are greater than those for the married. For white males, the likelihood of dying of heart disease between ages thirty-five and forty-four is two and one-half times greater for those who are divorced than for those who are married (200.0 to 81.1). In the above set of figures, married white females show the lowest rate, 11.8. Compare this with divorced white males, the group with the highest rate, 200.0. These divorced white men aged thirty-five to forty-four are seventeen times more likely to die of coronary heart disease than white females who are married and of that age. This great disparity is explained in good part by the stressful effects of the role of the divorced person and the male role, the less stressful effects of the female role, and the positive effects of the marital role.

Interestingly, death rates from coronary heart disease for married or divorced non-white males are lower than those for white males who are married or divorced. The picture is reversed, however, for hypertensive disease—one to which non-whites, blacks mainly—are especially vulnerable. For hypertensive disease, death rates per 100,000 persons aged thirty-five to forty-four years in the United States were:

	MARRIED	SINGLE	WIDOWED	DIVORCED
White Males	3.6	10.1	7.3	13.2
Non-White Males	48.4	84.8	134.0	112.3
White Females	2.8	5.2	5.1	5.0
Non-White Females	49.8	78.6	94.7	54.4

For each sex-race group, rates for married persons are definitely lower than for the single, widowed, or divorced. Male rates are, in general, greater than female rates. And non-white rates exceed white rates many times. Thus, married white females have the lowest rate, 2.8. Widowed non-white (low prestige) males show the highest rate, 134.0. This is forty-eight times as great as the rate for the married white females.

Of special interest is the tendency of young women who become widowed to die of coronary heart disease. Widowed females aged twenty-five to thirty-four years have a death rate from that disease over five times greater than that of married females of the same age. The discrepancy is not nearly as great for widowed as compared to married males of that age, but the same tendency is there. The discrepancy is also much less for males and females at older ages. Here are the figures:

Ratio of Death Rates of Widowed to Married Persons
from Coronary Heart Disease, United States, 1959–1961

	WIDOWED	
	Males	Females
15 and over	1.5	1.5
25–34	2.0	5.2
35–44	1.8	2.3
45–54	1.7	1.7
55–64	1.6	1.5
65–74	1.5	1.4
75–84	1.4	1.4
85 and over	1.4	1.6

Death rates due to cancer are also closely linked to marital status. As examples, death rates due to cancer of the buccal cavity and pharynx are 4.1 times greater for divorced men than for married men. They are 2.1 times higher for widowers than for married men. However, it is for tuberculosis, cirrhosis of the liver, accidents due to fires, and pneumonia that the death rates of the widowed and divorced most exceed those of the married. As the data below show, divorced white males are, in comparison to married white males, over eight times as likely to die of tuberculosis and about seven times as likely to die of cirrhosis of the liver, from accidental fires, and from pneumonia. Widowed white men, compared to their married counterparts are five times as likely to die of tuberculosis, four times as likely to die of cirrhosis of the liver or pneumonia, and seven times as likely to die from accidental fires.

Death Rates for Divorced, Widowed, and
Single as Percent of Death Rate for Married White Males,
Aged 15 to 64 Years, Standardized for Age, United States, 1959–1961

	MARRIED	SINGLE	WIDOWED	DIVORCED
Tuberculosis	100	485	529	876
Cirrhosis of Liver	100	291	461	752
Accidental Fire	100	246	733	658
Pneumonia	100	503	400	715

Suicide rates vary greatly according to marital status. Rates for the divorced and the widowed are several times greater than those for the lowest rate group, the married. Here are suicide rates per 100,000 population for males and females aged fifteen to sixty-four years broken down by race.

	MARRIED	SINGLE	WIDOWED	DIVORCED
White Men	17	32	92	73
Non-White Men	10	16	41	21
White Women	6	8	12	21
Non-White Women	3	3	6	5

Widowed white men are five and one-half times more likely to kill themselves than are married white men. Also, those widowed white men are thirty times more likely to kill themselves than the lowest rate categories, non-white women who are married or single.

As noted earlier, females are less prone to kill themselves than are males. Also, as the table shows, non-whites—largely blacks—have decidedly lower suicide rates than whites. The rage that blacks feel in the face of extreme stress due to role and other problems tends to take the form of aggression toward others—for example, homicide—rather than toward self, suicide. Whites tend to go in the opposite direction. Rates of commission of homicide by blacks are several times greater than those by whites.

Homicide victimization is also a measure of role stress. Persons under stress are more likely to come into contention and to get involved in lethal situations *either* as a victim or as an offender. Homicide death rates per 100,000 population for persons aged fifteen to sixty-four years by marital status, sex, and race are:

	MARRIED	SINGLE	WIDOWED	DIVORCED
White Men	4	7	16	30
Non-White Men	51	79	152	129
White Women	2	1	7	9
Non-White Women	14	17	33	25

With one exception, single white women, homicide victimization rates are greater for single, widowed, and divorced persons than for married persons for each sex-race category. Homicide death rates for unmarried non-white men are extraordinarily high and those for married and single white women are extremely low. Non-white men who are widowed have a rate 152 times that of single white women.

Finally, death rates due to accidents of all kinds vary widely according to marital role. Adjusting for age, accident death rates per 100,000 population are three times as high for divorced persons as for married persons and over twice as great for the widowed as for the married: married, 45; single, 87; widowed, 102; divorced, 131; all, 58.

Especially striking are the death rates from accidents of both males and females who are widowed at a young age compared to the rates for married persons of the same age. Widowed women aged twenty to twenty·four years have death rates due to accidents that are seven times those of their married counterparts. Widowed men of those ages have death rates five times those of married men of the same ages.

More and more it becomes clear that deaths due to accidents are seldom accidental. Rather, lethal accidents are frequently unconsciously motivated responses to high stress. Some have a large homicidal component, while others are distinctly suicidal. Research has shown, for example, that fatal single-car crashes have some tendency to be suicidally motivated, while fatal multiple-car crashes are much more likely to be homicidal.

6

Role Stress in the United States and the World

TWO EXTREMES: NEVADA AND UTAH

Broad demographic measures indicate that role stress is concentrated more in certain parts of the United States than in others. Some states have much more stable patterns of role relationships than others. The contiguous states of Utah and Nevada offer an interesting contrast. Utah is extremely stable in its way of life, due in good part to the deep attachment to the Mormon religion. Of Utah's adult residents, 63 percent were born in that state. For Nevada, the figure is 10 percent. Changing of residence within the states is 50 percent greater in Nevada than in Utah.

Nevada, of course, is known for its gambling and liberal divorce laws. Over 20 percent of Nevada's males aged thirty-five to sixty-four years are not living with marital partners. In Utah, the comparable percentage is but 10 percent. In Nevada in 1977, the overall rate for serious crime was 7,968 per 100,000 population. (For each 100,000 persons living in the state, 7,968 serious felonies were officially recorded during the year.) This was the highest rate for any state. Utah had a rate of 4,751, distinctly below the national average of 5,055.

The average lifetime of persons living in Utah from 1969 to 1971 was 72.9 years. Only two states had a longer average lifetime. On the other hand, Nevada possessed an average lifetime of 69.03 for its residents, ranking it fifth from the bottom among the fifty states.

Utah has the lowest infant mortality rate of all the states in the United States. The rate was 11.9 per 1,000 infants in 1974. Nevada has the third highest rate, 18.2 in 1974. Death rates at all ages are greater in Nevada than in Utah. For example, from 1966 to 1968, the death rate for persons aged forty to forty-nine years was fifty-four percent greater for males in Nevada than for males in Utah; for females of that age the death rate was sixty-nine percent greater in Nevada than in Utah.

Nevada has an extremely high suicide rate; Utah has a low rate. Nevada had the highest suicide rate of any state in 1974, 27.0 per 100,000; Utah ranked thirty-third with a rate of 11.0. Thus, Nevada had two and one-half times more suicides per unit of population than Utah. Nevada had the ninth highest homicide rate in 1974, the rate being 13.6 per 100,000; Utah ranked fortieth among the states with a rate of 3.7 per unit of population. Thus, Nevada had almost four times more homicides than Utah. Put another way, residents of Nevada are 3.7 times more likely to be murdered than are residents of Utah.

One cannot, with any certainty, make direct linkage between these indicators of stress and specific role problems in the two states. Nevertheless, the likelihood is exceedingly great that in Nevada the absence of stable family relationships and the rootlessness and the transiency that necessarily involve losing roles and taking on new ones contribute considerably to personal and social stress. In contrast, the relative absence of transiency, the stability of the family and other role relationships, and the commitment to the religious role, all moderate role stress to a significant degree in Utah.

THE STATES OF THE UNITED STATES

David L. Dodge and Walter T. Martin have developed an ingenious method of measuring role stress in the states of this country. They determine, specifically, the amount of role conflict that is prevalent in a population. They do this by measuring the extent to which individuals do or do not occupy roles commonly associated with each other. For example, in the United States, it is common for physicians to be males and uncommon for them to be females. If, in a given state, a relatively high proportion of physicians were females, that would be taken to contribute in a small way to a high level of role conflict and of stress in that state. If a very low proportion of physicians were females, that would be taken to contribute in a small way to a low level of role conflict and of stress in that state. Roles that are commonly carried out by the same persons are considered to be relatively unconflicted and to create low stress conditions. Those rarely carried out by the same persons are considered to be highly conflicted and stressful.*

In Table 6.1, death rates for each of three groups of states are given: states with low, medium, and high levels of role stress.† The 16 low stress states combined have an annual death rate from heart disease of 423 per 100,000 population. For the 16 medium stress states the rate is 492 and for the 16 states in the high stress category, 578. Hence, the high stress states have thirty-seven percent more deaths from heart disease per unit of population than the low stress states. Of interest is the fact that Dodge and Martin found Nevada to have the highest stress level and Utah to have the lowest stress level.

There is much evidence that links at least some common forms of cancer with stress. The Dodge-Martin research, also Table 6.1, shows that the annual death rate per 100,000 population from malignant neoplasms for the low stress states is 121; for the medium stress states, 135; and for the high stress states, 158. The cancer death rate, then, is 31 percent higher in the high stress states than in the low stress states.

Similar findings were made by Dodge and Martin when they took, one by one, thirty-one states for which data were available and compared death rates from various other diseases with measures of role stress.‡ They report a correlation of .80 between arteriosclerotic heart

---

*Dodge and Martin use the term status integration. Status refers to the position associated with the role and integration refers to the extent to which statuses (roles) are commonly found to go together.

†Here role stress is measured in terms of how common it is for individuals of either sex and of different ages to hold various marital statuses.

‡Here, as above, role stress was measured in terms of the commonness of individuals of either sex and various ages holding the several marital roles. Dodge and Martin used inverted measures of stress; these have been converted to direct measures.

Table 6.1   Annual Death Rates from Heart Disease and Malignant Neoplasms per 100,000 population for Persons Aged 55–64 Years, by Role Stress Levels of States of the United States, 1950

| | ROLE STRESS | | |
	Low	Medium	High
	Arkansas	Alabama	Arizona
	Idaho	Colorado	California
	Indiana	Georgia	Connecticut
	Iowa	Louisiana	Delaware
	Kansas	Michigan	Florida
	Kentucky	Minnesota	Illinois
	Mississippi	Missouri	Maine
	Nebraska	Montana	Maryland
	New Mexico	New Jersey	Massachusetts
	North Dakota	North Carolina	Nevada
	Oklahoma	Ohio	New Hampshire
	Oregon	South Carolina	New York
	South Dakota	Tennessee	Pennsylvania
	Texas	Vermont	Rhode Island
	Utah	Washington	Virginia
	Wisconsin	West Virginia	Wyoming
Death Rates:			
Heart Disease	423	492	578
Malignant Neoplasms	121	135	158

SOURCE: David L. Dodge and Walter T. Martin, *Social Stress and Chronic Illness*, Notre Dame, Ind.: University of Notre Dame Press, 1970, based on data from pp. 123 and 126.

disease deaths and role stress levels; of .76 between deaths due to malignant neoplasms and stress; of .70 between cirrhosis of the liver deaths (often due to excessive drinking) and stress; of .48 between diabetes mellitus deaths and stress; and of .29 between leukemia deaths and stress. (The last has a strong genetic component and often occurs in the young, not subjected to role stress as measured in this research.) The first three correlations are quite strong. The correlation of .80 means that about two-thirds (64 percent) of the variations in the arteriosclerotic heart disease death rate of the states can be predicted from the levels of role stress in the states.* For malignant neoplasms, 58 percent of the variations in the death rate can be predicted from the stress level; for cirrhosis of the liver, 49 percent; for diabetes mellitus, 23 percent; and for leukemia, but 8 percent.

*Predictability is determined by the square of the correlation figure.

Evelyn M. Kitagawa and Philip M. Hauser present data that link socioeconomic differentials among the states with death rates. They found the following correlations between death rates for males and females aged twenty-five to sixty-four years and three indicators of socioeconomic levels:

	MALES	FEMALES
Median Years School	−.48	−.52
Median Family Income	−.31	−.28
Percent Black	.75	.83

These figures mean that there were moderately strong negative correlations between death rates of males and females and years of school completed: the more schooling, the lower the death rates. There were weak negative correlations between death rates and income: the higher the income, the lower the death rate. There were strong positive correlations between death rates and the percentage of blacks in the states' populations: the greater the proportion of blacks, the higher the death rates.

COUNTRIES AROUND THE WORLD

Societies around the world differ enormously in the role stress levels that their populations experience. They also vary greatly as to resources for coping with stress and as to the medical facilities for treating the disease consequences of stress. Using suicide as one measure of role stress, one can see in Table 6.2 the wide variation from societies such as Hungary, with annual suicide rates of forty-one per 100,000 population, to others such as Kuwait, Mexico, and Kenya, which have very little suicide.

By most measures, role stress is quite high in the United States as compared to countries generally. The mortality rate for males in the United States who are under the age of fifty-five years is double the rates for Sweden, Norway, or Denmark. The coronary heart disease death rate for United States males aged thirty-five to sixty-four years is six times that for Japan (400 per 100,000 population as compared to 64 per 100,000 population).

Another good measure of role stress is life expectancy. For coun-

Table 6.2 Suicide Rates in Literate Societies, Circa 1972

Hungary	40.7	Channel Islands	11.4	Spain	4.2
German Dem. Rep.	36.6	Poland	11.3	N. Ireland	4.0
Denmark	23.8	Hong Kong	11.1	Ireland	3.5
Austria	23.6	Uruguay	11.1	Greece	3.4
Finland	23.5	Singapore	10.3	Guadeloupe	3.4
Czechoslovakia	22.4	Iceland	10.2	Guatemala	3.4
Bahamas	21.4	Puerto Rico	9.1	Ecuador	3.2
Sweden	20.8	New Zealand	8.8	Panama	3.0
South Africa	20.1	Norway	8.7	Colombia	2.9
Germany, Fed. Rep. of	19.9	Portugal	8.6	Cape Verde Is.	2.8
Switzerland	18.8	Scotland	8.4	Peru	2.2
Japan	17.5	Netherlands	8.2	Barbados	1.7
Belgium	15.6	Trinidad/Tubago	8.1	Paraguay	1.5
France	15.4	England & Wales/UK	7.8	Philippines	1.1
Luxembourg	13.0	Reunion	6.9	Angola	1.0
Bulgaria	12.7	Italy	5.8	Jamaica	1.0
Canada	12.5	Venezuela	5.5	Kuwait	0.8
S. Rhodesia	12.2	Chile	5.4	Mexico	0.7
United States	12.2	Israel	4.9	Kenya	0.2
Cuba	11.9	Mauritius	4.6		
Australia	11.6	Costa Rica	4.2		

SOURCE: *Demographic Yearbook,* 1974, New York: United Nations, 1975.

tries around the world for which data are available, the average life expectancy for those born in 1972 is 55.2 years—53.9 years for males and 56.6 years for females. For those born in the United States, life expectancy is 72.4 years (68.5 years for males and 76.4 years for females). Quite a number of countries have longer life expectancies than we do. The leading ten are:

	MALES	FEMALES
1. Sweden	72.1 years	77.4 years
2. Norway	71.2 years	77.4 years
3. Netherlands	71.0 years	76.8 years
4. Iceland	70.7 years	76.3 years
5. Denmark	70.7 years	75.9 years
6. Japan	70.5 years	75.9 years
7. Israel	70.1 years	72.8 years
8. Spain	69.7 years	75.0 years
9. Canada	69.4 years	76.5 years
10. Switzerland	69.2 years	75.0 years

The ten countries with the lowest life expectancies for those born in 1972 were:

	MALES	FEMALES
1. Guinea	25.0 years	28.0 years
2. Gabon	25.0 years	45.0 years
3. Chad	29.0 years	35.0 years
4. Togo	32.0 years	38.5 years
5. Upper Volta	32.1 years	31.1 years
6. Central Africa	33.0 years	36.0 years
7. Guinea-Bissan	33.5 years [a]	
8. Angola	33.5 years [a]	
9. Bangladesh	36.0 years [a]	
10. Nigeria	37.2 years	36.7 years

[a] Males and females combined; not reported by sex.

Of course, these low life expectancy countries are ones where role stress is not a primary cause of short life. Starvation and inadequate diets, poor health conditions, and rampant communicable diseases are major problems leading to death.

David L. Dodge and Walter T. Martin have devised measures of role conflict for countries of the world just as they have for states in the United States. They find quite clearly that the higher the role conflict, and therefore role stress, the higher the death rates from cancer and heart disease. Of twenty-eight countries, fifteen were classified as high and thirteen were classified as low on role stress. They were then classified as having high or low death rates from malignant neoplasms.

Table 6.3 shows that twelve of the fifteen high stress countries had high death rates from malignant neoplasms. And eleven of the thirteen low stress countries had low death rates from malignant neoplasms. When role stress scores and actual death rates from malignant neoplasms were compared for the twenty-eight states, the correlation figure was .72.* This means that 52 percent of the variation in death rates among the states could be predicted from their role stress levels. Dodge and Martin made a similar analysis of heart disease death rates and role stress levels for the twenty-eight countries. They found a correlation of

*Role stress was measured in terms of the commonness of persons of either sex being in the labor force. As before, Dodge and Martin used an inverted measure of role stress; this was converted to a direct measure.

.50. Twenty-five percent of the variation in death rates in the states could be predicted from their levels of role stress.

Table 6.3 Countries Above and Below the Median with Respect to Malignant Neoplasm Mortality Rates and Measures of Role Conflict (Labor Force Status with Sex)

	HIGH CONFLICT	LOW CONFLICT
High Malignant Neoplasm Mortality Rates	Ireland Yugoslavia Canada New Zealand England and Wales United States Sweden Finland West Germany Switzerland Austria Denmark	Union of South Africa Australia
Low Malignant Neoplasm Mortality Rates	France Belgium Japan	Netherlands Mexico Guatemala Costa Rica Greece Chile Ceylon Norway Israel Portugal Hungary

SOURCE: Based on data from David L. Dodge and Walter T. Martin, *Social Stress and Chronic Illness*, Notre Dame, Ind.: University of Notre Dame Press, 1970, p. 284.

II

THE SOURCES OF STRESS

7

Conflict within a Role

THE PROBLEM

This and the next six chapters are concerned with the social psychodynamics of role stress. The ten major sources of stress outlined in Chapter Two are: conflict within a role; conflict between two or more of a person's roles; conflict between the roles of one person and those of another person: overdemand in a role; underdemand; restrictiveness of roles; role loss; taking on of new roles; role rejection; and encroachment by others on one's roles.

One of the most common of these sources of stress is conflict within a single role. Here there are conflicting demands—that is, expectations by others—as to how one should properly carry out the role. If the person meets certain expectations in the role, then others must necessarily go unmet. It is ultimately a no-win, a "damned if you do and damned if you don't" situation for the individual. Most of us have learned a need to meet our role demands. If conflict causes us to fall short of meeting some of those demands, we are likely to experience an underlying fear that others will disapprove of us, blame us, or withhold rewards. The fact that the role is inherently conflicted does not necessarily act as a mitigating factor. We are likely to feel that we *should* carry out the role effectively even if conflicting demands make that all but impossible. The more we clearly understand the nature of role conflict the less likely we are to experience self-blame and fear, and the more likely we will be to innovate some ways of coping with this "double-bind" type of role problem.

Everyone experiences minor role conflicts from time to time. Often we resolve them easily as we go along. You are going to be very late for an appointment because an earlier one took far longer than anticipated. You call ahead, explain the situation, and make amends in advance. All is well. Severe problems arise, however, when role conflict continues over months or years without resolution. Stress is likely to mount and in the long run to be debilitating. A number of everyday roles generate just such long-term conflict and stress. The foreman in industry, the waitress, certain executive roles, and the police officer—these are all classic examples of work roles with built-in conflict. Each is a role that has demonstrably stressful effects.

Notice that these roles are always at the meeting point between two groups with quite different needs. The foreman stands midway between management and labor. The waitress is the woman in the middle, between customers on the one hand and restaurant cooks and staff on the other hand. The police officer is caught between those who demand law and order and those who want to violate the law and disorganize the order. (Often those who demand law and order want exceptions made in their own cases.)

Why is this form of role stress so common and why are so many of us unable to cope with it effectively? As noted above, we are often unaware of the problem. We know we feel poorly or that we are exhausted, but we do not connect that to the role. We may blame other persons who are making conflicting demands upon us, not seeing that the problem is basically the role rather than them. They, in turn, then become annoyed and aggressive with us and the situation is worsened. Further, the stress brought about by role conflict causes us to become anxious, to tighten up. This tends to make us go on doing, compulsively, whatever we have been doing. It blocks off constructive coping.

THE FOREMAN

The foreman's role is found in most industrial and business organizations and in others that get work done as well. The foreman is the first-line boss, the one who actually sees to it that others do their work. Each industrial shop or section of a shop has its foreman. In business, office managers are often equivalent to foremen. Head salesman, chief cook in a large restaurant, department chairperson in a college or university, police sergeant—these are all essentially foremen. In the military, sergeants and in some instances warrant or petty officers and lieutenants are the foremen. Traditionally, foremen have been males. Increasingly, however, they are women—especially in business office settings.

The basic conflict for the foreman is the one between the demands of management and those of the workers. Management expects, above all else, that the foreman will maximize the productivity of the workers under him and see to it that running costs and waste are minimized. Workers expect the foreman to further their interests, to take their side against management, and to avoid pushing them to greater and greater work output. They expect the foreman to make things easier, not harder, for them. After all, from their point of view, he *is* one of them. He *was* a worker who was promoted. Management, on the other hand, sees the foreman as their representative on the front line.

As a result, stress in the foreman's role runs high. In the Tennessee study of 130 occupations, the foreman's job ranked sixth from the top in stressfulness. The office manager's job ranked fifth. A few thrive on the tension caused by conflicting demands and the challenge of coping with them. Many find the game not worth the candle and return to a non-supervisory work role. Others stay in the foreman's role, find the resultant stress highly burdensome, become irritable, "difficult to live with," and may develop such psychosomatic symptoms as severe headaches and ulcers.

If the foreman faces conflict and overdemand in his other roles, especially familial roles, stress is compounded and can well lead to a breakdown. On the other hand, if stress in the foreman's familial roles is not high, he may well be able to sustain the cross pressures of the job without undue harm.

It is exceedingly difficult for the foreman to reduce stress in the work role per se. Often he arranges other spheres in his life so that lower levels of stress thus counterbalance the high stress on the job. One foreman who had a rewarding and not especially stressful family life nonetheless felt the strain of the job pervading his life generally. Gradually he evolved a hobby that provided an outlet for the stress of his work role. He had for many years played the saxophone. In his youth he had for a short time been the organizer of a three-piece band. Now, he got together some friends, also musically inclined, and they formed a band. They played first at community get-togethers without a fee.

This man and his band now play paid dates three evenings a week and on weekends. His wife often accompanies him. His income has increased considerably. He is doing something he loves to do. Above all, playing music seems to make the tension that he develops on the job melt away. In addition, he has a sense of not being so dependent on his foreman's job. He could make his living with the band if he had to, he feels. He did not consciously set out to ameliorate the effects of his work role in this way, but that is what he has done and quite effectively too.

There are, however, certain ways in which the foreman can learn to cope directly with the stresses of the job. The first, as always, is to understand the dynamics of the role. He must see that it is an inherently conflicted role. He must understand that the problem lies not in particular other people who are "bugging" him and not in his inability to meet the role's demands. Rather, the problem lies in the inevitably different goals of management and labor and in the consequent conflicting expectations upon the "man in the middle."

The foreman must learn that he is a mediator, that if he helps each side to get half a loaf he will receive more praise than blame. After all, both management and labor want more than half a loaf and he is the link between them. For the foreman to arrange things so that each gets a loaf is impossible. The two sides must settle for less than they demand or the role would break apart and thus would no longer be the vital link between management and labor.

Consequently, the effective foreman who survives—who does not get results at the expense of greater and greater stress—sees that he is a mediator and an innovator. He must devise ways of finding common ground between management and the workers. He must help each to achieve their goals to some degree without blocking the goals of the others to too great an extent. *That is why he is there.*

If he can innovatively accomplish that, the foreman will have met the conflicting demands of the two sides each about halfway. That is what he is *really expected* to do. Put differently, management and labor each have an implicit second set of expectations that the foreman will meet their demands (first set of expectations) only partially. For doing so he will be rewarded.

THE WAITRESS OR WAITER

Conflict in the waitress or waiter role can be almost as severe as in the foreman role. In the Tennessee study of stress in 130 occupations, the waitress (and waiter) ranked eighth from the top. Stress arises from the conflicting expectations of customers, cooks, and management. The customers want prompt, pleasant service and good food. The cooks want the waitress or waiter to explain away to the customers the fact that one order of food is insufficiently cooked, that another is overseasoned, or that a third is unduly delayed. Owners or managers want the waitress or waiter to provide efficient service, to serve rapidly so that there is a good turnover of tables, and to smooth over any complaints and disgrutlements of customers. They are the people in the middle, trying to negotiate between these several parties—especially cooks and customers—who do not know or see each other. If they slight the customers, their tips go down. If they jump on the cooks, they are likely to become recalcitrant and make their job harder—say, keep the customers waiting—and this too can lead to less tips. Again, some waitresses and waiters are very good at coping with the built-in conflict of these roles. Others, a majority, find their work hectic and stressful. This is one reason they change jobs so frequently. They seek a less conflicted situation, thinking that the stress they have encountered is peculiar to that particular restaurant, cooks, management, and customers. There is seldom awareness that the central problem is one of inherent role conflict.

Waitresses and waiters are prone to psychosomatic disorders, peptic ulcers in particular. They have death rates well above average for employed persons as a whole. (Death rates from specific causes have been systematically collected in a number of studies on male waiters, seldom on waitresses.) Rates of death from cancer of the buccal cavity and pharynx are two and one-half times higher for waiters than for males in all occupations taken together. Deaths due to arteriosclerotic heart disease and other myocardial degeneration are one and one-half times as likely among waiters as among employed men generally. Also, waiters die of influenza and pneumonia about twice as often as other men.

Of course, there are other sources of stress in the waitress and waiter role. Many find it demeaning to serve others food in an egalitarian society. Others find it demeaning to be pleasant to customers, not out of genuine feeling, but simply to gain good tips. Waitresses and waiters who find basic reward in this work tend, however, to feel that they are performing important rather than demeaning work. They see the job, in good part, as one of mediating between customers, kitchen, and sometimes management as well. Rather than experiencing frustration because they cannot always fulfill the demands of all parties involved, they gain a sense of reward by smoothing over difficulties.

THE PRESIDENT

Some executive roles in business, industry, and government are further examples of work roles with high levels of internal conflict and therefore stress. However, these vary according to the particular type of executive role. In the Tennessee study the middle range executives in business and industry ranked seventh from the top in stressfulness. Interestingly, very high level executives usually do not find their roles as stress-inducing as those below them on the organizational charts. The company president is often beholden to the Board in a technical sense but in many ways he is likely to be one of them and they may well follow his lead. Thus, his role is not in conflict with those above and below him. However, executives at lower levels are necessarily caught, to some extent, between the conflicting demands of their superiors and subordinates. Moreover, the president or chief executive officer is likely to be a highly resourceful person who can cope with conflict and stress situations, otherwise he would not have gained the role in the first place. Also, in many cases, he has great resources of power and funds that further allow him to cope effectively.

The role of president of the United States is the epitome of the executive role fraught with conflict. He is beholden to numerous interest groups that hold sharply conflicting expectations of the presidency. So do different wings of his own political party, the members of other parties, the Senate, the House of Representatives, the judiciary, the members of his staff and cabinet, and even the leaders and interest groups of foreign nations.

The president is continually at the center of myriad cross-cutting conflicts, and the public expects him to see that these conflicts are sufficiently resolved so that the society can function. For the most part he designates individuals to do this, but the society views him as ultimately responsible.

Most individuals would be unable to cope with the stress of the presidency for a few days, much less for years. The long series of primaries, the nominating process of the political parties, and the presidential campaigns themselves serve to weed out those who do not thrive on high conflict. As a consequence, practically all presidents have been men geared to cope with and withstand extreme role stress, especially from conflict and overdemand. Of course, the society accords them great power, in part so they can use it to resolve conflicting interests. Nevertheless, many have become ill in office or have died soon after leaving office as the result of stress. Woodrow Wilson is a paramount example. Lyndon Johnson and Franklin D. Roosevelt are two other good examples.

THE POLICE OFFICER

The police officer's role takes a heavy toll in high incidences of health and behavioral problems. Police forces hire only men in good physical condition. Yet police officers suffer from heart disease, hypertension, and back trouble to a much greater extent than those in most other occupations. In general they die younger than men in most lines of work. Specifically, they are twice as likely to die of diabetes mellitus and arteriosclerotic heart disease than are all men in the United States. They have a suicide rate that is almost twice the average rate for men in all occupations. They are more likely to die because of one or another of those three reasons than men in *any* other occupation.

Further, police officers are more than twice as likely to be homicide victims than men in general. Only about a third of this is due to being murdered on the job. Much of their homicide victimization occurs in off-duty hours when they become involved in altercations with relatives, friends, or acquaintances. They have high rates of depression and alcoholism. One good measure of alcoholism is death due to cirrhosis of the liver. Police officers are 64 percent more likely to die of this disease than men in general.

Conflict is the main reason for stress in the police role. The most central source of stress is the conflicting expectations of the public. Some want a harsh "law and order" crackdown on offenders, while others want more and more leniency. Again, many of the same individuals insist that the law be enforced even-handedly, that the police officers play no favorites—except when it comes to them and members of their families and their friends.

There are many other sources of stress in the police officer's role: Officers with very weak educational backgrounds, who were hired years ago, now find it highly threatening to be told that they must pass a rigorous training program. Police officers often prosecute cases in court; this puts them at a tremendous disadvantage in relation to law school trained defense counsels and judges. Police work can be extremely undemanding, routine, and boring one hour and exceedingly demanding and complex the next. Such abrupt shifts cause stress. Moreover, police officers are involved in a rapidly shifting variety of interpersonal relationships—with persons in distress, serious criminal offenders, petty traffic offenders, juvenile offenders, court personnel, and so on—which require training and skills in communication, negotiation, and conflict resolution which most officers do not possess. Police officers often see the worst side of human nature in their work and that in itself is likely to be stressful. They are exposed to much violence, to individuals criminally wounded and killed, and to death and woundings due to accidents. The fact that they may become "hardened" to this only testifies to the underlying stress involved. Finally, the police officer witnesses much illegality and corruption by other police officers. It is well established that police officers have high rates of assault (without sufficient cause), of collusion in theft, of bribe-taking, and the like. They are very seldom prosecuted and the relatively honest officer must accept the criminality of his fellow officers, must himself violate the law by failing to report a crime, or must lose his job.

The stress of police work carries over into the family. The officer is often emotionally frayed and may well release his anger at home. Divorce rates are high. Officers and their teen-age children are frequently in severe conflict. The natural inclination of youth to rebel against authority may be just too much for the officer after coping with that out on the beat day after day.

On top of all this, police officers are exceedingly prone to finding retirement stressful. Few police departments have adequate procedures for insuring gradual retirement. For years the officer is involved in a highly conflicted and demanding role. Then suddenly he is retired, and he finds it very difficult to adjust to the change. The conflicts and demands are gone. Their absence and the consequent decompression can be extremely stress-inducing.

Many police officers believe in a vague, general way that their role is fraught with conflicting demands. However, they are likely to feel that they ought to be able to handle them, to handle the job—any part of it. They often hear the stereotyped macho image of the adult male described as a person who should be able to cope with any stressful situation within his usual sphere of life—the John Wayne image, as one psychologist has called it. Seldom does the police officer fully grasp the fundamental reason for role stress mentioned earlier: Society wants police officers who seem to uphold the law at every turn but who really do so selectively, who close their eyes to some violations by certain individuals and prosecute others vigorously. Officers know, of course, that some politicians and some influential citizens take this view. However, they are likely to conceive of them as the unusual ones. Rarely do they comprehend that social values in general are thus. True, not all of us share in those values—but those are the prevailing ones. This basic conflict in values and social expectations pervades the police role, racking it with conflict, making high demands, and providing scarcely any adequate training.

There are, of course, officers who thrive on the conflicts and demands of the police role. They have developed in such a way that they require high levels of stress. However, they are few and far between. Most suffer the various distresses and ills mentioned earlier. In the long range sense, two things need to be done. First, change the police role so it is less stressful. This means decreasing the underlying conflict in social values. Secondly, provide vastly greater and more effective educational and vocational training for police work. However, these are very long-

range goals and they bear little on the realities of a given officer's immediate problems. For the officer who is under severe stress, the problem
is a very difficult one. As long as he stays in his present job he is very
likely to experience the same family problems and the same health
and behavioral symptoms. Yet, he very likely has no skills—no
qualifications—that would allow him to enter another line of work.
What is he to do? One recourse is to seek a less conflicted variation of the
police role either within the force or in private employment. Desk officers and dispatchers are subjected to less stress than patrol officers.
Positions as security guards in the private sector are usually far less
conflicted than those of municipal police officers. One problem here is
that many officers find the idea of shifting to one of these positions
threatening to their sense of identity; a "cop-out."

A small percentage of officers will be able to go back to school in
their off-duty hours and train for another occupation. Others will suffer
through the stresses and strains of their work as best they can. Some will
become ill and will either be retired early or dismissed. For those who
have no career options, one of the most promising paths toward the
reduction of role stress is the guided group therapy session. Some departments, recognizing the severe toll that police work takes, have
begun to institute these. Officers in groups of six to ten meet weekly
with a psychiatrist or psychologist who is highly familiar with police
work. On the one hand, they relieve tension by expressing their frustrations and seeing that they share the same problems—are in fact all in the
same boat. On the other hand, they can come to comprehend conflict
and other sources of the role stress they experience and how those lead
to health and behavioral disorders. Understanding a role stress problem
can help enormously in reducing its harmful effects, even if one cannot
modify or abandon the role. Once one knows clearly the nature of the
problem, one tends automatically to shift one's behavior and attitudes in
small, gradual ways that at least in part reduce and ameliorate stress.
This is far from an ideal solution. It is also far better than none at all.

The foreman, the waitress or waiter, the president, the police
officer—these are, then, examples of roles with severe built-in conflict.
They are all work roles. It is in the world of work that this form of
conflicted role tends to develop as a mediating mechanism between
groups with divergent interests and goals. A person would do well to
consider ahead of time whether a given occupational career or a particu-

lar job is inherently likely to involve conflict, and if so whether one is geared to coping with this form of stress.

It is important to note that we rarely, as a society, consider changing a work role so that it is less conflicted. (It is also true that we seldom consider changing any roles that are sources of high stress.) We think in terms of changing individuals rather than roles. Even then the emphasis is not so much on devising ways of helping people to cope more effectively with role stress. Rather it is on getting them, in one way or another, to tolerate—to make do—with the stress. Of course, a given innovative person may be able to change a conflicted role for himself or herself sufficiently to ameliorate some of the stress problem. However, this is far different from changing the role in the general sense.

For example, the police officer's role is simply too stressful, for the reasons given above. It needs to be fundamentally changed. In England the police officer's role has traditionally been a respected one, and far less conflicted than here. Police officers in England are not beholden to local political control to nearly the extent they are here. They are not expected to carry out as many non-police functions there as here. They are much better trained. The English have been a people given to abiding by the law, to rule following. They do not expect the law to be bent in their individual favor to the extent we do.

Our police role needs to be changed so that it is more professionalized, so that training is vastly improved, so that non-police functions are reduced, and so that it is removed as much as possible from direct local political influence and control; then the police role would be challenging rather than debilitating. Able persons would be more likely to make police work a career. We would all be better off for the change.

8

Conflict between Roles

Apart from conflicting expectations for a single role, there are two forms of conflict between roles that frequently engender stress. The first involves conflict between two or more of a person's roles. The second has to do with conflict between the role of one person and the roles of one or more other persons. This form is discussed toward the end of this chapter. As to the first, here a person has two or more roles which are such that if the expectations for one are met, then the expectations for another cannot be—at least not well. Job and family roles often conflict in this way for husbands-fathers and for working mothers. Sex and work role may conflict, as in the case of the female firefighter or the male secretary. Again, there may be value conflict between the two roles, as in the case of the devoutly religious man who is expected, in his business executive role, to use ruthless methods toward his employees and his competitors.

WORKING MOTHERS

One of the most familiar examples of conflict between a person's roles is the working mother. In this and most societies, role expectations for the female have been and are that she will marry in late adolescence or early adulthood, will bear children, and will raise them and care for the home. Recently expectations have also developed that the woman will hold a job outside the home as a symbol and a fact of emancipation, as well as to increase the family income. However, no special provisions have been made to lighten the burdens of caring for the children and the home. Thus, the woman is likely to be "damned if she does and damned if she doesn't." If she stays in the home she is seen as being out of step with the "modern" image of a woman. If she puts everything into a career—does not marry and have children—she may well be seen as a selfish shrew. If she is a working mother she may find it nearly impossible to meet the role expectations of wife, mother, and worker simultaneously. The time and energy required on the job draw time and energy away from meeting expectations in her family roles. This is especially the case if she is the mother of young children, since there are strong expectations that she be with her children "when they need her"—which means much of the time. On top of all this, her husband may have been reared in an environment that leads him to expect that his wife will not hold a job outside the home.

If the young mother stays in the home with the children, she not only fails to meet expectations that she work. She also consigns herself to a highly restrictive environment, one that at times may be extremely demanding and at others may be undemanding and boring. Conversely, if she puts total emphasis on a career, she not only fails to meet expectations that she be a wife and mother. She very likely will miss dearly the support of marriage and the intrinsic rewards of raising children.

Indications of changing patterns in job roles provide one avenue toward resolution. The increasing emphasis on flexible work hours is a promising form of change. Several studies have clearly shown that when women can choose their work hours and rearrange them as necessary, the stress of role conflict abates significantly. Gaining some control over *when* one carries out conflicting roles can be an important means of ameliorating stress.

Some married couples have been able to make arrangements whereby husband and wife each work half-time. In rare cases they have even been able to share the same job—some teachers, for example. However, for most people these solutions are not feasible. It will be a long time before flexible work hours are common in most jobs for women or for men.

If a woman truly prefers work in the home to an outside job, there is no intrinsic reason why she should not remain in the home. If stress then arises it will probably be due to the expectations of others that she will work outside. She would do well to confront the issue squarely and convince herself that her expectations for herself are, in this instance, what are critical and that the expectations of others can, to some degree at least, be discounted. After all, those others are not literally going to take any severe action against her. The most they will do is voice mild disapproval, and if so they are likely to give that up before long.

Working mothers, working fathers, and in fact everyone with role stress problems must try to recognize that role expectations are just that—role expectations. Every time we fail to meet them we do not necessarily bring the wrath of others down on us. We have been conditioned since childhood to react automatically as if they will. True, failure to meet certain role expectations can have very negative consequences. This is the case when others are especially threatened by the non-conforming behavior. However, much of the time one can safely ignore role expectations. The important thing is to understand the difference.

A working mother may be able to piece together an arrangement whereby her pre-school child is in kindergarten three mornings a week, is in a day-care center two mornings a week, has a baby-sitter at home three afternoons a week, goes to a friend's home one afternoon a week, and is at the mother's place of work on Friday afternoons when things are slow. This may seem complicated, but the main issue is whether it works. Some may frown on having the child go from pillar to post, but no more than a frown will result. Moreover, the arrangements may be constructively stimulating for the child. However, if the mother were, out of desperation, to leave the child alone at home part of the time or to intrude the child into the work situation during much of the week, then more or less severe negative sanctions of others might well come into play; so might the mother's negative evaluation of her own actions.

The moral is a simple one, really—but often very difficult to put into effect: Figure out ways around role problems that are not harmful to relevant parties, not unduly threatening to them, and yet accomplish the end of reducing role stress.

THE PHYSICIAN

Any work role that demands much time and energy and over which one has little control is likely to come into conflict with one's family roles. The physician's role is notorious for this. Most physicians spend great amounts of time in their offices and at the hospitals. Their work demands concentration. While they may become somewhat inured to it, there is always the stress of working in the midst of illness, disease, and death. Most doctors have to strain to summon up the energy and arrange the time to carry out their husband and father (or wife and mother) roles adequately. Wives resent this, often bitterly. Moreover, physicians tend to exercise authority in all their relationships—no doubt because this is to some extent demanded in their work role. They are likely to attempt to closely control the behavior of their wives and children, although they see little of them. This leads to conflict between their husband-father roles and the roles of their wives and children, a third type of conflict to be discussed shortly.

While rewarding in prestige, money, and a sense of doing important work, the physician's role is, then, a highly stressful one. As a consequence, doctors as a group suffer from a variety of personal problems and disorders, many of which the public is only now becoming aware. Despite the stereotype of the physician as very nearly omnipotent, doctors are no better equipped than highly educated and prestigious people in general to cope with other than medical problems. As evidence of this and of high role stress, physicians do in fact have high rates of divorce, alcoholism, drug addiction, and death from arteriosclerotic heart disease, diabetes, and suicide.

A telling case of role conflict between a doctor's roles is that of William H_____, a highly respected general practitioner in a mid-sized city in the Northeast. Forty years old, he had gone to Harvard Medical School, had married his childhood sweetheart during his senior year as a medical student, and now has two children—a boy twelve and a girl ten. His patients liked him, had much confidence in him. He was popular with the other doctors and the hospital staff.

One day just before Christmas, Dr. H. disappeared. He left no message. No one, including his wife, knew where he was. The other doctors in the community tried as best they could to take over his patients. Two weeks later H. was found in an obscure hotel in New York City. He had been there the entire time. He was in an amnesic state. He remembered nothing of leaving his family and patients or of the intervening two weeks.

The other doctors were concerned that H. had abandoned his patients. So was H. himself. The county medical society quietly investigated the matter. The only explanation was that H. had suffered an amnesic reaction. But why? A few doctors mentioned overwork. However, while H. worked hard, almost always putting in a twelve to fourteen hour day, that was not uncommon. Many of the doctors did the same. A few of the other doctors were close friends of the H.'s. They knew H. and his wife had not been getting along especially well during the last few years. But, as one of them said, "My God, there's nothing very unusual about that."

H. himself could give no explanation. His health had in general been good. He had, he admitted, felt increasingly rushed and under pressure the past year or so. H. shrugged the whole thing off and continued to practice as before. The county medical society quietly closed the investigation.

The interesting thing is that no one—not one of the physicians, not H. himself—emphasized the connection between the amnesic state and a critical, central fact of H.'s life during that period. He had been increasingly caught in a bind between his professional role and his husband-father roles. Because of the hours spent at the hospital, at his office, and on emergencies, he was seldom at home. His wife grew to complain bitterly. What was the point of it all, she said, if she was at home all the time, if the children hardly knew their father, if there was never a time together, never a vacation? Both of them had worked so hard to make ends meet during his last year in medical school, his internship, and the first years of practice. Now they had plenty of money, but for what?

H. could not understand why his wife complained. She knew all along what a doctor's life was like. She had had no complaints the first years he was in practice. Something had happened to her, he thought.

She had become a terrible crank—a shrew, really. At the same time, he had to admit that he seldom saw the children—didn't want to see them, really—because he grew more and more tired in the evenings, had all he could do to keep going. Being with the children only tired him more; so did any discussion with his wife.

Yet H. felt he should be with his children more often, much more often. He and his wife should get along well. They certainly had in the earlier years. What was wrong with her? He didn't know. He should know. He was a doctor. What was wrong with himself? He felt increasingly under terrible pressures. He liked his work, really, but he was—it was true—neglecting his family. He was becoming more and more irritable, unreasonably so at times. Then suddenly, through the onset of amnesia, he withdrew from the conflict both physically and psychologically.

Doctors in some communities have partially solved this family-work role conflict by caring for each other's patients one day a week so that each can spend some time with his family, usually at a second home where they cannot be reached. Others have moved into medical roles with regular hours and without ongoing responsibility for patients—pathology and anesthesiology, for examples. The important thing is for the doctor to assess the role conflict situation realistically and to attempt to ameliorate it. Ignoring it or simply trying to live with the strain almost invariably means trouble ahead.

CONFLICT IN AGE ROLES IN MIDLIFE

Conflict between changing age roles is still another important source of stress. At certain junctures in the life cycle, the demands of the age role one is leaving and those of the age role one is taking on are, to some extent, mutually exclusive. Further, the new role may be threatening because it is demanding (early adulthood) or because it is undemanding (old age).

For many of both sexes the midlife transition can be the most painful of all role stress experiences. The person is leaving the active early middle-aged role, taking on the less active later middle-aged role, and beginning to prepare for old age. The illusion of immortality rapidly dissipates. Fears of senility and death are common.

For the male, role demands in the thirties and forties often are for vigorous action to achieve occupational success—that is, greater responsibility, social standing, and financial reward. (This is true of blue-collar workers as well as white-collar workers and professionals.) For the female there are the conflicting role demands to be a competent wife, mother, and working woman. For both sexes there are the demands to "make the marriage work," to raise the children responsibly, and frequently to take an active part in community life. The thirties and the forties are a time of struggle for "happiness."

For the male in his very late forties and early fifties, role demands are directed toward consolidation of gains, a judicious approach to life, the use of ability within a work role (often one of diminishing responsibility), rather than achievement of higher status, and gradual preparation for still further reduced activity in the sixties and seventies. For the female in the same age range there is, even more than for the male, the necessary to adjust to the loss of the everyday, active parental role as the children move to full independence and to the *physical appearance* of being older.

The thirties and forties, then, are years when role demands are for ascending responsibility, while in the fifties demands are for backing off, consolidation, and eventual decrease in responsibilities. It is in good part the conflict between these two sets of age role demands, plus fear of the future, that leads to crisis around age fifty. (For females, normal changes during the menopause may affect reaction to stress.) The dividing line between the two life stages is not firmly drawn at a very specific age by social convention. Each person is expected, within certain bounds, to work it out for himself or herself. This leaves, for most, a time of great ambiguity and uncertainty. Interestingly, many persons would be spared much severe stress in midlife if role demands were more clearly delineated by age in years.

So many of us, not in all societies but certainly in ours, want to retain the familiar younger age role, and this impedes us from meeting the expectations of others for the unfamiliar older age role. How are we to cope effectively with this dilemma? Those who do so tend to conceive of life as a never-ending process of gradually making transitions in age roles rather than in discrete age periods. They are likely to plan carefully for those transitions. They retain an inner sense of youth while adjusting to society's role demands for aging and to the physical realities of aging. They grow old youthfully.

CONFLICT BETWEEN
TWO PERSONS' ROLES

When we clash with others, very often it is because our roles clash, and we are seldom aware of that. When roles of different individuals are in conflict they are striving to fulfill mutually exclusive role expectations. Each gets in the other's way. So each is likely to be antagonistic toward, and to blame, the other. Almost any competition involves this form of role conflict: workers competing for promotion, salesmen competing for sales, students competing for grades, politicians competing for power, and neighbors sometimes competing for prestige through displays of conspicuous consumption.

Conflict between the sexes, especially in marriage, is one of the most common forms of this type of conflict. Expectations as to how adult males and females in this society are to act in relation to each other have become ambiguous. It is not clear whether the traditional roles of courtesy apply. In some circles women resent a man holding a door or giving up a seat for them; in others they welcome it. At more important levels, hiring practices in business, industry, and academic life now sometimes give preference to women where once males were preferred. In sports, females are moving into roles traditionally held by males only: race car driving, for example. Women news reporters are in the male athletes' locker rooms, although the reverse is seldom the case. Women hold governmental positions of much authority and responsibility. In Great Britain a woman is prime minister for the first time.

All this brings the two sexes into competition for power and authority, prestige and esteem, and income as never before in western countries. Ambiguity over which sex has which rights under what conditions heightens sex role conflict. When these problems are fused with problems of marital role conflict, as is now the case, conflict within the family intensifies. What rights does the husband have? The wife? What are the obligations of each in insuring the rights of the other? In the sexual realm, is the female still the less dominant, less the initiator of sexuality? Who is to care for the children? Who is to take care of the home? Who is to work outside the home and at what? Who is to handle family finances? How are husband and wife to divide responsibility for children, home, and earning income?

Thus, marital role expectations are in many quarters of the society no longer clearly delineated. Yet the marital relationship is and has been the most intimate, complex, and difficult to carry out of any human relationship. No other relationship demands such long-term meshing of two individuals' needs and behaviors.

For marriage, then, individuals take on the most complex of roles, usually with very little preparation. The previously noted changes in sex roles—superimposed on the marital roles, as it were—complicate the process still further. The consequences are negative, often extremely so. One in three marriages now ends in divorce; and where divorce does not occur there may be long-term separation. The breakup of an unsuccessful marriage can be as stressful for the partners, not to mention the children if there are children, as the marriage itself—sometimes more so.

The marital role relationship becomes the lightning rod for tension developed in other roles. Much of this derives from our striving for higher social class standing—that is, for roles of greater and greater prestige. We strive to achieve the education to get the job to gain the money and marital goods that symbolize prestige. Stress in the job role or other problems in achieving prestige are likely to increase tension in the marital role. So are problems internal to the family. Difficulties in rearing the children often put strain on the marital relationship. Even questions of how to spend leisure time can lead to marital tension. Of course, sexual problems between husband and wife can also be another basic source of stress.

The man and woman who have agreed to spend their lives together, to help each other with life's problems, and in most cases to share in the rearing of a new generation, are beset by myriad, confusing, and often conflicting expectations about what they should do in order to be "adequate" males and females, in order to have a "healthy" sexual relationship, in order to be "in love," in order to raise their children "properly," in order to achieve a "suitable" income, in order to be socially acceptable consumers and displayers of material goods—including dress and housing, and in order even to recreate acceptably. In other words, there are thousands upon thousands of demands upon married couples to measure up to what others expect of them.

In so many marriages husband and wife run and run to achieve these expectations of others. That the expectations may be unreasonable or unsuitable for the given individual's needs is seldom even considered. They must have a new car (or two new cars), a house of such-and-such a type, clothes that meet certain specifications of others, a sexual relationship that is "honest" and "rewarding," children who do well in school, and so on. The mass media drum these expectations into married couples and potential husbands and wives day and night. Individuals may take all this so seriously that they literally experience severe stress because of fear that their grooming and dress do not reflect the "ideal" expectations demanded by the mass media and the advertisers.

Marital couples, and just about all of us whether married or not, in fact, are so programmed to accept the necessary of meeting role expectations of all kinds, no matter how outlandish, that we seldom stand back and ask ourselves whether given expectations make sense for us. It is so often in life that the husband and wife are supposed to meet these expectations *jointly*. Failure to do so means frustration, stress, and often a tendency to blame the other spouse and to become aggressive toward him or her. This is a central reason for the failure and breakup of marriage.

While couples may have suffered much marital role conflict, divorce for most means added stress because of sudden change, loss of role, and dislocation of the family. As noted earlier, divorced people die at an earlier age than married persons and are more prone to heart attacks and cancer. They have high rates of alcoholism and suicide. In addition, divorced men are eleven times more likely to be hospitalized for mental illness than married men and divorced women five times more likely than married women. Divorced men are eighteen times more likely to be confined to jail or prison than married men; divorced women are five times more likely to be confined than married women.

Yet in the United States and many other countries there is no explicit preparation for taking on marital and parental roles. The time and effort put into preparing for an occupational role is often prodigious; but we assume that people will know how to carry out the marital and parental roles. They seldom do. Their main role models are their parents, who also had no training for those roles. Other information comes from fictionalized, romanticized, distorted, and oversimplified accounts in the mass media.

If one wants to take on a role satisfactorily, logically one would study the role carefully, analyze it, consider one's relevant abilities and disabilities, consult with successful players of the role, and practice the role. Doing those things before marriage is likely to meet with derision and hostility. The conventional wisdom holds that marriage is a purely personal affair that must be worked out after it is launched upon—and largely behind closed doors.

ROLE CONFLICT WITH THE MACHINE

Machines can be very efficient, if simple-minded, role players. Except when malfunctions occur, they can carry out various tasks precisely, according to expectations, time and again. In the future we humans will interact with machines in role relationships more and more. If we do not understand the roles of machines, then relationships between them and us will become especially ambiguous. Lack of clarity as to what we and they are to do in response to each other may readily lead to severe conflict between our role and the machine's role.

If some find the idea of human role playing depressing, they may view the discussion of the role of the machine as even more depressing. That very nicely illustrates one of the problems of roles as a means of providing human social organization. It is fairly easy to design or program a machine to carry out a very rudimentary role. While more difficult, it is also possible to program a person to perform a role like a machine. We do so all the time. Many machines are simplified versions of human role players, often with one or more characteristics emphasized—the gigantic hand of the derrick, the rapid calculating ability of the computer.

Machines are used more and more in place of instructors for teaching languages. They guide the student, give rewards and punishments for correct and incorrect learning, make corrections, and so on. Aircraft automatic pilots and landing devices can fly a plane from take off to landing—except under certain emergency conditions. (Problems arise when it is unclear to the pilot whether he or the machine should be in charge.) Machines monitor patient treatment in hospitals. In one instance it was eventually found that patients had been receiving dangerous overdoses of cobalt treatment for cancers for more than a year. The machine that measured the treatment had been administering these overdoses of cobalt regularly. No one had the role of monitoring the machine because the machine was believed to be too efficient to require that. And we are all familiar with the computer systems in businesses that overbill us, send us threatening notes, and contact the computer at the central credit bureau which then blacklists us as a bad credit risk if we fail to meet their expectations.

These examples illustrate the problems we face because we have not addressed the issue of the role of machines in our lives—of their roles in relation to our roles. Until we do address this, machines will have more power over our lives than necessary. For example, we now see the computer as a thinking machine that accomplishes "mental" tasks beyond our abilities. Since we view it that way, it has that effect. Actually, a computer is simply a machine that carries out very simple tasks with great accuracy (usually) and rapidity. A computer can compute nothing that humans cannot compute. It simply makes computations with much greater speed than humans are able to do.

We should conceive of computers as filling assistant roles in various work situations. We are in charge and they are very junior workers with little range of activity and small scope for creativity, but with a true flare for almost instant calculation. Computers may find such an approach to them rewarding. Setting expectations too high for computers causes them "role stress" because of overdemand. Their circuits overload and they suffer breakdowns. Interestingly, electric shock treatment (extra surges of power) may then be necessary in order to get them working again.

9

Overdemanding Roles

OVERDEMAND IS RELATIVE

A demanding role is one in which expectations are considerably greater than the individual's preparation, abilities, and motivation to meet them. The central focus here is not on roles that are stressful because of conflicting demands, or because they are restrictive, or because of other reasons. Here we are referring to a role being stressful centrally because the level of performance is beyond the person's ability to produce. Cases of people getting promoted "over their heads" are good examples. They are simply not equipped to do the job.

Regarding all sources of role stress—conflict, overdemand, underdemand, restrictions, role gain, role loss, rejection, or encroachment—the degree of stress is to some degree relative to the individual's needs and abilities. This is especially true when a role is stressful because it is overdemanding. Individuals differ considerably from one another in mental, physical and emotional abilities and training, as well as in needs. Roles vary greatly in the physical, mental, and emotional demands they make and in the training they require. Consequently, what is an enormously demanding role for one person may be hardly so at all for another.

Of course, people tend to gravitate to roles that are not excessively demanding for them. Also, for certain roles—especially work roles—there may be recruitment criteria that screen out many who are unlikely to be able to cope with the given role's demands. However, people make mistakes in choosing roles, recruitment processes are far from infallible, and sometimes we are forced into roles whose demands are much too great for us. Further, it may be next to impossible to rid oneself of an overdemanding role. For example, a young woman may want to marry, bear a child at an early age, then a second, and then twins. She may end up rather quickly with more children than she can manage—with a severely demanding parental role.

Then there is that well-known Peter principle: Workers tend to be promoted to their level of incompetence. Many an able person has been promoted and given a large salary increase only to find that the new position makes demands that he or she cannot meet, or at least not without extreme expenditure of mental and emotional energy. To request demotion, a cut in responsibility and salary, is in our society almost unthinkable.

When role demands upon us are too great in our everyday lives, we become anxious or we begin to suffer from one or several symptoms: headaches, dizziness, backaches, abdominal pains, feelings of depression, and so on. Also, it is well established that persons under extreme work demands tend to aggress verbally against members of their families as ways of reducing tension.

While any type of role may be overdemanding for some individuals, it is often work roles that are most so. Some jobs are simply physically taxing. Many men in the construction trades and in longshoremen's work find their jobs extremely so. The role of air controller, to be discussed shortly, is very demanding emotionally. Students sometimes find that their roles demand mental abilities that they do not have.

Illustrations of persons with inadequate training or education are found in many "high-powered" business executive roles. Men in those jobs who lack a college education show distinctly higher rates of stress-induced heart disease, psychosomatic symptoms, and alcoholism than their college graduate counterparts. The verbal skills learned in college play a significant part here. So does the fact that in present-day business settings executives who lack a college education are at a disadvantage socially. Poise, assurance, and proper use of language are really parts of the demands of the job.

Research studies have shown that the single best predictor of the number of years men will live is the degree of satisfaction or dissatisfaction with their jobs. The greater the dissatisfaction, the less the longevity. This does not mean, of course, that job dissatisfaction is a killer per se, but it is certainly associated with shortness of life and probably contributes to it. Also, job dissatisfaction applies to more than the stress of overdemand in a job. It can apply to the stress of role conflict in the occupational setting and also to that occasioned by undemanding jobs.

However, overall there does seem to be a definite causal relationship between job dissatisfaction, as brought about by overdemands, and health. The more demanding the job, the higher the rate of mental disorder and alcoholism. Those in overdemanding jobs are significantly more likely to be affected by coronary heart disease. One study analyzed the relationship of coronary heart disease to various specialties within three occupational categories: medical doctors, dentists, and lawyers. There was almost a perfect correlation between levels of stress and rate of coronary heart disease: The more demanding and stressful the specialty, the greater the rate of heart disease.

AIR CONTROLLER

The air controller's job is exceedingly taxing in an emotional sense. It also requires mental quickness and agility. It can also be stressful in the physical sense, since work shifts for a given controller are often irregular and yet may be scheduled close together. There are too few controllers for the increasing volume of air traffic. A given controller is often responsible for fifteen to twenty aircraft at a time. Equipment is outdated and frequently malfunctions. Jurisdictions are unclear in many large urban areas so that an aircraft is passed from one controller to another without adequate coordination and communication.

The basic source of stress for controllers is, of course, the fear that aircraft under their control will collide or crash, that numerous individuals may be killed or maimed, and that they may be blamed. They do difficult work under adverse conditions and if a crash occurs there may well be ambiguity over whether the responsibility lies with the controller or elsewhere. Hence, he or she can readily feel an impending sense of failure to fulfill role expectations of a life-and-death nature.

Air controllers suffer from insomnia, ulcers, and hypertension. They have nightmares about crashes. They have a high divorce rate. Heart attacks are far more frequent than the national average. Interestingly, the rate of heart attacks among controllers is six times that for airline pilots. It is little wonder that work stoppages and strikes are common among controllers in this and other western countries. They are trying to signal alarm over their own stressful situation and over an increasingly dangerous problem for the public. These actions have the further functions of removing them from the direct source of stress for a time and of providing them with a symbolic form of aggression—the refusal to work.

This is a good example of a stressful work role that requires extensive modification. It is not the controllers who should adjust to the role. It is the role that should be changed. True, if controllers are able to avoid undue stress in other areas, such as family roles, they will be better able to withstand the stress of the job. However, this role stress problem will never be fundamentally resolved until more funds are made available to employ more controllers so that each controller is responsible for fewer aircraft; until jurisdictional lines for controlling aircraft are made less ambiguous; and until more effective communication and other equipment, already available, is installed nationwide. This will require a clear recognition that these factors contribute both to harmful effects of stress on controllers and to aircraft accidents and deaths.

OVERDEMAND IN THE STUDENT ROLE

Countless students are pushed by parents or others beyond their abilities in elementary and secondary schools and in college and professional schools. Very likely many of these young people have the fundamental mental ability to do the academic work, but they have not, for one reason or another, learned the necessary intellectual skills. Some rebels, of course, drop out of school. Many try to measure up to the role expectations of family and friends, find the strain intolerable, and later experience the stress of role failure as well.

Sam R_____ is a fairly typical example. In high school he was an open, happy-go-lucky young man. He and his parents got along well. A star basketball player, he was well liked by his teachers and peers. The school's standards were not high and his grades were reasonably good. His father was a pharmacist who had aspired to medical school. He desperately wanted his son to be a doctor. Sam's mother agreed. They saved every penny they could for his future education.

Sam was easily admitted to the state university. The first semester his grades were three D's and two C's. His parents were shocked. He was bewildered and disheartened. He had never really had to study to earn B's in high school. So he had never learned how to study. He was a slow reader; he wrote poorly. His attention span was short. While he was not certain about medicine as a future career, he knew clearly that he wanted to complete college. He gave up playing on the freshman basketball team, the only part of college he actually enjoyed. He diligently applied himself to his studies. At the end of his second semester he had earned three C's and two D's. His parents could not understand it. At first they thought he was "running with a party crowd." Finally he convinced them that this was not so. They then thought there must be something wrong with him physically. During the summer they had him thoroughly tested at a nearby clinic. He was physically very fit.

During the fall semester Sam spent nearly all of his time studying. He managed five C's. He did not want to let his parents down. He found the premedical curriculum a rigorous one. He applied himself tenaciously. His grades never rose above a C+ average except for one semester when he had an easier course load and achieved a B− average. By his senior year Sam had lost much weight, had a pained and harried expression, and suffered from recurring severe headaches and frequent nausea.

Sam applied to twenty-two medical schools. Most did not even ask him for an interview. He was rejected by all. He was terribly depressed. His parents were disbelieving. He had a C+ average, he worked hard, he was a fine young man. And one medical school after another rejected him. His father went so far as to go and talk with the associate dean of one school, a man he had known earlier in his life. The dean said he would give it to him straight. The boy simply did not have it for medicine. Some people did and some did not. There were many fine young men and women who had A– averages, even A averages, who were rejected for medical school these days. If you had only a C+ you had no chance whatsoever.

The moral is that we should be extremely careful in setting expectations as to what roles those close to us should carry out: The young person is unable to have the resources and autonomy to innovate a way around stressful role overdemands. Hence, if the young do not rebel and instead diligently try to meet those demands, they are very likely doomed to mental or physical breakdown, to failure in the role, or possibly to later effects of that failure in the form of a negative self-image.

THE FOOTBALL PLAYER

College and professional football players, especially linesmen, will sometimes tell of the physical and other stresses of their roles. College football is a big time business, as is its professional counterpart. There is enormous pressure for top college players to play, regardless of illness or injuries. Many linesmen take drugs before a game that give them a prolonged high and markedly decrease their sensitivity to danger and pain. Opposing linesmen, not on drugs, are at a decided disadvantage.

With or without drugs, players often find themselves pushed beyond reasonable bounds of strength and endurance. They are injured and play with those injuries, aided by further doses of painkilling drugs. The coaching staff wants desperately to win. The college administration or the professional team owners have much at stake. The public wants strenuous action—combat, really—regardless of the consequences. The players themselves want to win and to attain stardom. All this is intensified by the mass media.

On top of the sheer physical demands, players are expected to assume the role of super jocks: not very bright (with a certain stumbling speech), insensitive to the aesthetic and intellectual aspects of life, and so on. As a college player wrote, "Ever since I was thirteen or so, people have expected me to be physical, not mental. They have expected me to be able to take anything because I was big, because they needed a big linesman. They have acted as if I couldn't be expected to know anything, but that as long as I went out there and produced—really made a difference for the team—it didn't matter."

Football players do not like to talk about the stresses of their role. Talk of having to play with extremely painful injuries, of having to use the head as a battering ram against opposing players (which can cause permanent brain damage even with the helmet), and of drug taking, only alienates coaches and management. Admitting their feelings only threatens their own sense of role, of self, of supposedly being able to withstand and endure physical stress.

We have, then, a social role that is stressful because of physical demands and also because of expectations that the player will submerge the self and become the super jock. The role feeds the big business interests of college administrators, professional team owners, and the mass media. It also meets the needs of those members of the public who want to see others endure stress. True, the star player receives adulation and, as a professional player, monetary rewards. He is not dragooned into being a player. There comes a point, however, at which a society should reassess the fundamental significance for the quality of life of all its members of roles that have especially deleterious effects on a few.

10

Undemanding and Restrictive Roles

UNDEMANDING ROLES

Compared to most societies around the world in the past or present, ours is an especially competitive and demanding society. Many of our roles are conflicted and overdemanding. We yearn to be free of the tensions that these produce. We sometimes think how nice it would be just to dawdle along, as the spirit moves us, without having to do this or that—without having to measure up. Certainly a mixture of demanding and undemanding roles can be salutary. The undemanding roles, often avocations, provide a welcome relief from the "pressure cooker" roles.

However, the desire for less pressure tends to block our understanding of the fact that undemanding roles can be exceedingly stressful. They bring about stress in an inverted way. The absence of challenge and the lack of opportunity to achieve—these engender boredom. Boredom is stressful. Basically, boredom connotes an absence of stimulation. This can be as harmful to us as overstimulation and conflicting stimuli.

It is true that escape from roles of any kind may, at least under certain conditions, be beneficial. However, carrying out an undemanding role is not beneficial. The role is there. It *requires* that we do little in relation to our abilities and inclinations. As with restrictive roles, undemanding roles put a damper on our needs to express ourselves and to meet challenges. A related reason why undemanding roles lead to stress is this: Since most of us have learned to need to exert ourselves to meet the demands of roles and thereby to gain rewards and avoid punishments, we may feel apprehensive when the demands of a role fairly central to our lives are easily met. We are so geared to striving to meet role expectations that our bodies react with alarm if few role demands are made on us.

No one thrives on across-the-board lack of challenge. For a person with several highly demanding roles, however, having an undemanding role to turn to may be a welcome relief. The problem is one of balance. It is when an undemanding role is central to our lives or when our waking hours are made up largely of carrying out several undemanding roles that we grow bored, apathetic, and experience a terrifying sense of nothingness that comes from following a simple, unchallenging routine day-in and day-out.

BUREAUCRACY AND ROLE STRESS

Modern social life is, in considerable part, organized around bureaucratic structures. Government, the military, big business and industry, public education—these are the major forms of bureaucracy. They form what many people refer to as "the system." It is here that the average person is able to conceive the nature of roles most clearly. In bureaucracy, work role demands are singularly impersonal, designed to achieve certain ends—regardless of the particular needs of individuals. The worker in the bureaucracy may be derogatorily labeled by others as "a true bureaucrat" who frustrates their attempts to get what they want. However, they recognize that the person did not start life that way, that the bureaucracy made him or her that way.

The difference between the bureaucratic role and other roles is that the bureaucratic role has been consciously designed by someone or some group, while the others—such as those in the family—have not.

There are written rules and regulations and job role "specifications," in the bureaucracy which do not exist in other settings. However, the unwritten expectations of the housewife role, say, may be just as real as those of the professional soldier's role. They are simply not as visible, not as tangible.

Many workers in bureaucracy are required to do only routine tasks that present little challenge, little opportunity to use their abilities. Bureaucracies usually have built-in controls that discourage and punish attempts to increase the demands of work roles. Rate busters are penalized and ostracized. Those who suggest innovative procedures are ignored or shunted aside. The essence of bureaucracy, coercing individuals to act out narrow role demands—regardless of individual differences and needs—is preserved.

There is an important exception to what has been said. Some leadership roles in the bureaucracies are extremely demanding. They may be highly conflicted as well. Heads of government agencies, military commanders, business executives, and in some cases educational leaders may be under extreme pressure—that is, demanding role expectations—to produce certain results. Their roles may be in much conflict because of the demands of one part of the bureaucracy as against another or because of the demands of the public in relation to the bureaucracy.

INDIVIDUAL DIFFERENCES AND UNDERDEMAND

As with any form of role problem, there are considerable differences among individuals. Because of past experience, formal training, personality, physical condition, and the nature of one's other roles, what is terribly undemanding and therefore stressful for one person may provide a considerable challenge or welcome diversion for another. There was, for example, the vivid case of a middle-aged woman who worked as a tester in a plant that manufactured electric light bulbs. Every few seconds she picked up a bulb from the conveyor belt and pressed it to the current to be sure it lit. The company decided to diversify the work of its employees in order to reduce boredom. She was taken off her regular job four out of five days of the week. She grew extremely upset and agitated. Each time a bulb lit she saw a new and beautiful, exciting scene. Those scenes formed a central part of her life. Now they were taken away from her, except for one day a week.

Roles that once provided some challenge and were in some degree constructively demanding may, of course, become dreadfully boring. In most such instances it is not that the role changes. It is that we change. We become so proficient at carrying out the demands of the role that its challenge generally dwindles to a very low level.

It is a common phenomenon that people whose lives are dominated by one undemanding role or another strive to inject some stimulation into those roles and their lives generally. They get into contention with others over minor matters. They take risks, often self-destructive ones, in order to roil the stagnant waters of boredom. They seek out demanding leisure time roles. While these strategies can be successful, all too often they get us into serious trouble and serve only to increase our stress load.

On some automotive assembly lines it is common to see men who put the same bolt in the same place on car after car every thirty seconds scream obscenities at visitors walking on the catwalks alone. The use of drugs, as a way of escape from the terrible routine, is not unusual. Sabotage is common: for example, throwing loose metal in a section of the car to be sealed off. Workers in humdrum bureaucratic jobs are well known for making life miserable for members of the public they serve: for example, the endless rejecting of forms that are never properly (according to hidden regulations) filled out. Bored middle-class housewives sometimes engage in shoplifting as a form of risk. They seldom realize that the central underlying dynamic may be whether they will get away with it or whether they will be apprehended. The elderly in "Sunset Villages" may get into severe contention over such issues as the height of street curbs or the color of coverings for the furniture in the lounge.

Research findings on undemanding roles demonstrate the harmful stress they can cause. Robert Kaplan made an intensive study of twenty-three occupations representative of the total span of work roles. He found the three most undemanding and boring occupations to be assembly line work, machine tending, and operating a fork lift. Workers in these jobs experienced more psychosomatic complaints and depression than workers in any of the other jobs, including highly conflicted and overdemanding ones. Interestingly, the more education workers have the greater are the negative stressful effects of jobs usually classified as undemanding. Workers with less education find them somewhat more demanding, less boring, and therefore, less stressful.

Undemanding jobs are not in general associated with high death rates. The stress takes its toll in various psychosomatic illnesses—certain forms of severe headache and backache are examples—and in feelings of hopelessness and depression. Two exceptions in regard to death rates are suicide and death due to cirrhosis of the liver, which tend to be high for workers in some highly routinized, undemanding jobs. Severe depression can lead to suicide, and alcoholism as a way of attempting to cope with depression can result in cirrhosis of the liver.

SUDDEN SHIFTS IN ROLE DEMANDS

Some of us are afflicted by the stress that comes from sudden alternation between role demands that are excessively high or excessively low. This may be within a role central to our lives or it may occur as we shift from one central role to another over the days, weeks, or months. The effects of sudden alternation in role demands between very high and very low can be likened to compression and decompression. The pressure around one changes rapidly and it is exceedingly difficult for the body to adjust. This is experienced by submarine crews shooting to the ocean's surface during escape from a damaged vessel or by airplane crews when their craft's interior suddenly loses much pressure at high altitude. Sufficiently high or low levels of pressure will always be fatal. However, given time, one can adjust to considerable extremes of pressure.

Much the same is true in everyday social life. Too abrupt a shift in role demands from one extreme to the other can be extremely stressful. Of special interest is the fact that migraine headaches are often associated with the lulls that follow periods of intensive effort. Here again individuals vary considerably in their tolerance levels. Some can accept shifts in role demands that would tend to immobilize others, and some of us actually learn to thrive on such alternation in role demand. The compression and decompression may provide jolts to our physiological and psychological systems that we come to need.

In any case, most of us must either guard against rapid shifts in the demands of one of our roles or from one to another of the roles we carry out or suffer harmful stress consequences. The roles of police officer and fire fighter are examples of roles with built-in shifts in demand levels. One hour they may be engaged in complex, demanding, and dangerous tasks and the next hour they may be engaged in the most undemanding routines. This is one of the reasons that these two work roles are especially stressful.

Again, some alternation between high and low role stress is beneficial. We need periods of exertion and repose. The sameness of any condition over a long period of time is in itself stressful. An undemanding hobby may be just the relief required from an overdemanding job. However, too often we are unable to bring about the optimal alternation between demanding and undemanding roles. We may not be aware of the problem. If we are, it may be exceedingly difficult, require much innovation, to effect change. Innovation is hard to come by when one is beset by too many demands or the ennui that accompanies too low a level of demand.

THE AGED

It is an absolute certainty that an absence of adequately demanding and challenging roles contributes greatly to the plight of the aged in this and numerous other societies. Enforced retirement, lack of meaningful work, relegation to the far sidelines of life and being ignored by others—these play a large part in bringing on death. One of the major findings of Alexander Leaf's studies of three groups with especially high longevity is that the elderly carried out socially useful, prestigious roles until the end.

Very likely the problem is more severe for men than for women in the United States. Men retire from work in their sixties, and for too many the bottom then drops out of life. They may have held boring or otherwise stressful jobs, but for most men in our society any job is preferable to no job. Men in their fifties and sixties who are employed express considerably more satisfaction with their work than younger men. But older men who do not work, on balance, express much dissatisfaction with life. In any case, women are more likely than men to make a long transition into old age. At about age forty they lose the parent role, in the sense that they usually cease to act as a mother on a day-to-day basis, and that is likely to be traumatic. From that point on, however, women generally move much more gradually than men into the stressful condition of old age brought about by low role demands. Their situation is frustrating, but perhaps not quite as much so as that of males.

RESTRICTIVE ROLES

Roles are the way we organize ourselves, bring order to social life. They necessarily channel, delimit, and restrict our behavior. Yet the restrictiveness of our roles can be terribly harmful to us. It curbs our inclination to explore the world around us, to try out behaviors of various kinds, and to express ourselves freely—in a word, to be creative. The necessity is to achieve a balance between the social demands for conformity and the expressive needs of the individual.

Restrictive roles are as common in bureaucracy as undemanding ones. Individual expression and innovation are for the most part the enemies of bureaucracy. The aim of bureaucracy often is to have workers who behave as much like robots, and as little like unique individuals, as possible. Role expectations and rewards and punishments restrict the individual worker's behavior to very narrow channels. Any attempt to do things in a new and perhaps more effective way tends to be quickly punished, just as are the earlier mentioned attempts of a "rate buster" to do more than is prescribed.

While roles that are undemanding may also be highly restrictive, this is not necessarily the case. Some roles that demand considerable ability, time, and energy may be severely restrictive because of expectations of rigid conformity to rules and regulations. Workers in middle range positions in the giant governmental bureaucracies often experience stress because of this. So do career military personnel in peacetime.

Roles vary greatly as to their restrictiveness. Occupational roles range from many of the professional ones such as physicians, lawyers, and professors, which are relatively unrestrictive, to the bureaucratic roles, such as office workers, which are highly restrictive. Individuals show considerable variation in their tolerance of role restriction. Some of us have tailored our behavior to the demands of very restrictive roles for so long that we desperately need them, can barely function without them. (Many a long-term prison inmate, for example, becomes so habituated to the narrow confines of the inmate role that he simply cannot, upon parole, function in the somewhat less structured atmosphere of the wider society.) While some of us may grow to accept and to need highly restrictive roles, all of us who experience them—and that means most of us—are stunted by them.

The traditional roles of wife and mother have demanded a wide array of skills on the one hand and have restricted the female's activity on the other. The wife-mother has been expected to stay in the home and avoid a wide range of behavior. This is in part what many women are contesting now and these roles are gradually changing. The sense of helplessness and inner rage that comes from undue pressures to restrict one's behavior are likely to lead to depressive disorders. This helps to explain why in the United States and other countries depression has been far more frequent among females than males. Studies have found, not surprisingly, that the more flexible the housewife's role—that is, the more open to variation in routine and in self-expression—the happier women report themselves to be and apparently the less mental health problems they have.

Schools vary as to the restrictive nature of the student role. There is a central distinction between "progressive" and traditional schools. The former make less restrictive role demands on students. In most of our schools the child from the outset, kindergarten or first grade, is induced to fit into a mold of rigid behavioral demands. It is a common belief that the more that is done the better able the child will be to mature into a responsible adult. This is false. Children whose behavior is curbed to too great an extent become either rebellious or passive and apathetic.

Certainly the opposite extreme of relatively roleless situations for school children is equally harmful to them. They are given opportunities to express themselves to be sure, but they are denied the practice necessary for living in a world that is very nearly role bound. Children need roles of middle range flexibility and restrictiveness so that they can, to some degree, follow out their natural inclinations while also learning how to meet role demands. This is as true of the child in the family setting as in the school. However, a common tendency is for parents and teachers to fear that self-expression will lead to anarchy, and so they attempt to force children in the opposite direction.

THE NATURE OF UNRESTRICTIVE
ROLES

If roles are by definition more or less restrictive, then what is the nature of a relatively unrestrictive role? It provides guidelines for action, it prohibits certain behaviors, yet it allows for a wide range of alternative behaviors. An unrestrictive role provides a broad strategy for reaching some set of goals and leaves the specific tactics for doing so up to the individual. Experimentation and innovation are welcomed rather than tabooed, as is the case in restrictive roles.

The role of the research scientist is such. He or she who carries it out is expected to follow certain broad guidelines of science and ethics: use of the basic scientific method; no cheating—that is, falsifying—results; no actions clearly known to be harmful to subjects or others who might be effected, and so on. However, within such guidelines the whole nature of the scientist's role is not to do what others have done and stop there. The demand is to go beyond that, to create new knowledge—which is to say new ways of solving problems of all kinds, problems that range from how to harness nuclear energy to how to put humans in space to how to treat manic-depression to how to curb inflation.

Granted that highly restrictive roles can have reward value for some persons. They may especially need the security that can come from having their behavior channeled into very narrow limits so that they need to make few choices. The overriding fact, however, is that for the vast majority of workers in the bureaucracies the undemanding or restrictive nature of their roles, or both, cause much stress and take their toll in general well-being and health. Reasonably demanding roles that are relatively unrestrictive and allow considerable room for innovation—it is these roles that make life rewarding.

THE PRISON INMATE: ROLE
RESTRICTION AND UNDERDEMAND

Imprisonment is a matter of stripping away the convicted person's family, work, and other roles and replacing them with the highly restrictive and largely undemanding inmate role. Whether an inmate is married, widowed, single, or has children or does not is of little concern to the prison authorities and other inmates. There may be some interest in inmates' former work roles but unless they are ones that can be used in a prison (a male nurse would probably be set to work in the prison infirmary), they play little part in the day-to-day life of the prison.

The inmate role is such that there is a rule for almost any form of behavior. Some inmates are informally exempted from certain rules because they have been imprisoned for many years or because they are the leaders of prison cliques. However, most are required to conform to stringent rules or suffer severe penalties, such as deprivation of visitor and mail privileges or even solitary confinement. In many prisons the inmates must rise at a certain time in the morning, shave properly, put on regulation clothes, march to breakfast, refrain from conversation at meals, march back to the cell, clean the cell, march to the place of work, do the work (usually exceedingly routine), offer no suggestions, march to the mid-day meal, march back to work, march from there to the showers once a week, shower in view of the guards so homosexuality is controlled, be issued a weekly change of clothing, march back to work, march to the barber once every two weeks, march back to the cell, march to the recreation area for "yard time," and so on. No money is allowed, disrespect toward guards is not tolerated, mail and reading material is censored, and visitors to see inmates are screened and searched. Above all, the inmate is not expected to offer suggestions for change. Innovation is ruled out.

Many of these role expectations are not very different from those in the military. However, the military allows time off—passes and furloughs—so that duty is interspersed with periods of civilian life when military rules largely do not apply. For the prison inmate there is no escape from the continuous pressure to conform closely to myriad role expectations. During yard time many inmates work deals with other inmates to obtain alcohol, drugs, cigarettes, and food. They become attached to various inmate cliques and vie for influence and power over other inmates. From time to time riots erupt. These riots are largely a response to the stress of rigid role restrictions. They are especially likely to occur if the privileged ways of avoiding some of these restrictions that inmates have worked out are suddenly taken away from them.

Prisons do little to reduce crime. Most inmates have been there before; most who leave will return. This is in part because the inmate role is so restrictive, so destructive of individuality, initiative, and innovation that it not only fails to prepare criminal offenders for return to civilian life—it works against carrying out civilian roles successfully. At the same time, the one thing inmates have in common is experience in crime. They share and trade that experience and their knowledge of criminal activities. They informally teach one another how to commit crimes and strengthen one another's criminal roles so that those roles are likely to be stronger upon release from prison than they were upon entrance to prison.

MASS HYSTERIA IN THE FACTORY

The factory floor was incessantly noisy. The women worked at the various machines, turning out 1,800 pairs of men's work shoes a day. There were 290 women employed there. An additional 40 male workers moved the leather and other materials to the assembly lines, monitored the output, and oversaw the boxing and loading of the shoes.

Most of the women employed were middle-aged, earning little more than the minimum wage. They were at their machines all day except for a thirty-five minute lunch period and two ten minute breaks, one at midmorning, the other at midafternoon. The men were, in general, paid somewhat more and tended to be more mobile within the factory, to have jobs that required them to move around rather than tend a single machine hour in and hour out.

During the lunch break several of the women spoke to each other about feeling nauseous. Others mentioned that there was a blue haze in the air and that that might be causing the feelings of sickness. There was debate over whether there actually was a blue haze. At 2:30 one of the women vomited at her work place. Soon most of the women in that shop had vomited. The machines were shut down then by the supervisor. Women yelled about the "blue haze." The supervisor said he saw nothing. Women in other shops began to vomit. By 4:00 over half of the women employed at the factory had vomited or said they felt very ill. Only one man complained of being ill. The plant was shut down for the day and the workers sent home half an hour early.

The next day almost 30 percent of the women were absent. They felt weak, nauseous, and had severe headaches. Checks were made of the lunchroom kitchen and of the ventilation system because of the blue haze. No reason for the mass sickness was discovered. Soon things at the factory returned to normal. Five months later much the same thing occurred: women grew ill, felt nauseous, and suffered from severe headaches. Now it was summer and the outbreak was blamed on the excessive heat, although that day had been no hotter or no more humid than many other summer days.

Research by social scientists at the National Institute for Occupational Safety and Health has clearly demonstrated that restrictive work roles of an undemanding, boring nature generate temporary psychogenic illnesses, often nausea, in mass situations. High noise level in the work area is usually found to be present. Often there is a false belief that some condition in the physical environment—the air, the food, the water—"explains" the symptoms of illness. Working mothers are especially susceptible. Thus, role conflict may also play a part. The same phenomenon occurs in schools where students' roles are highly restrictive. Here it is not clear whether female children are more likely to be affected than male children.

11

Role Loss

FORMS OF ROLE CHANGE AND LOSS

The various forms of role change—modifying our existing roles, taking on new roles, losing or shedding of old roles—are further sources of stress. In any form of role change we must learn new behaviors or abandon old ones or, more usually, both. Further, when a role is lost or gained our other roles are likely to be affected. Getting married or divorced is, for example, likely to affect a person's work role; leaving a job, taking a new one, or being promoted or demoted may very well affect the marital role.

Role change requires behavioral change, and changing one's behavior can be—and often is—painful. However, it can also be challenging and rewarding. We are always in a process of role change, even when our roles seem very stable. Our age roles are constantly changing, and our other roles are likely to be shifting to some degree. While work roles, for example, may remain the same for long periods, more often there are gradual if not abrupt changes even in the same ones over the years.

Loss of roles is certainly one of the most traumatic and devastating forms of change and therefore one of the greatest sources of stress. Role loss occurs for a wide variety of reasons—some over which we have control, others over which we do not. The death of others close to us causes us to lose marital, parental, and friendship roles, as well as the loved ones themselves. We lose roles associated with age, as when the young adult must at some point abandon the student role and the elderly person the work role. Ill health may force us to give up roles at any age. Again, social convention may dictate the loss of a role. Enforced retirement, even though the individual is fully able to work, is a case in point. Role loss may be due to the decision of another, as when one is fired by the boss or divorced by a spouse. It may be voluntary: We give up one job for another; we seek early retirement; we initiate divorce proceedings. Moving to a new town or city, for whatever reason, usually involves loss of work role, friendship roles, and various community roles.

Certainly, new roles often replace lost roles. Also, we may lose roles that we dislike, are glad to be rid of, as well as those we value. Such matters, of course, affect the stress consequences of role loss. However, the overriding fact is that most forms of role loss result in considerable or more stress, initially if not in the long run.

THE TRAUMA OF ROLE LOSS

When loss of roles accumulates for a given person over a short period of time, the result is almost always devastating. An example of this is when a man's wife dies, his only child marries and leaves home, and he loses his job because of a recession. If several such role losses occur over, say, a single year, severe consequences are likely to ensue. Obviously, in certain cases of role loss due, for example, to the death of a spouse or of one's child, the surviving person suffers a double loss—that of the loved individual as well as that of the role. Research shows that most of us initially find the loss of the person more stressful than the loss of the marital or parental role. However, as time goes on, we tend to adjust to the loss of the person, while the stress of the lost role continues.

Why is the loss of the role so extremely traumatic? Roles are possessions; they are part of us. We are used to them. We have, as a rule, tried to tailor our behavior to meet role expectations. As has been emphasized throughout this book, we have been rewarded for doing so and punished for failing to do so. Leaving a role means adjusting our behavior to its absence. If the lost role is soon replaced by a new one, it necessarily means shifting gears, often abruptly. If the old role is not replaced, there is the necessity to adjust to the vacuum that is created. We must shift to neutral in that area of our life. Loss of a role is likely to mean vague or strong apprehension. The familiar is gone; we must attempt to cope with the unknown.

From childhood on roles are major mechanisms by which we erect structures of environmental support for ourselves. We get help from others and resources from the society through roles as son or daughter, as student, as marital partner, as worker, or as community member. Suddenly take away a person's critical roles in the family, at school, at work, and in the community and the person may very well collapse because his or her environmental support system collapses.

Of course, from an objective standpoint, many role losses do not necessarily mean loss of help from others and of resources from society. However, almost all of us have lost critical roles at one time or another, roles that did lead to a sudden drop in environmental support and so made us highly vulnerable. Therefore, we are likely to unconsciously associate the loss of any role, for almost any reason, with that earlier traumatic form of role loss.

Further, certain role losses—especially those brought about by the death of a loved one—make us feel helpless. We feel an utter lack of control. We feel there is no way we can repair the loss. This sense of helplessness can also later be unconsciously associated with role losses that are not so central to our lives, even that are in themselves welcome.

The symptoms of stress due to role loss can take many forms. Among the most common are feelings of depression (sometimes alternating with high anxiety) and even suicidal attempts and actual suicide in the face of very severe losses. Hypertension and heart attacks are common physical outcomes. Use may be made of alcohol and other drugs in attempts to alleviate feelings of acute discomfort. Extensive risk-taking may be resorted to in a desperate attempt to recoup a loss. When there seems to be no one directly to blame for the loss, it is not unusual for the person to engage in self-blame. The aggression one feels is directed somewhere—at the self. Helplessness turns to self-rage. In an oblique sense, the person is "taking control" by placing blame somewhere, however unrealistic. On the other hand, if we rightly or wrongly perceive other persons as responsible for our role losses we are likely to blame them and to vent our aggression toward them either psychologically or physically.

MEASURES OF STRESS
DUE TO ROLE LOSS

Thomas H. Holmes, a psychiatrist at the University of Washington, has developed a scale that indicates the extent to which various changes in life conditions generate stress. Many of them have to do with the loss of roles or the taking on of new roles. Some are changes that people generally view as undesirable; others are ones that most of us see as desirable. In the Holmes' scale, the highest possible stress score is 100 and the lowest is zero. A glance at the scale will show that eight of the ten leading stress inducers involve loss of roles of one kind or another. In the first three the marital role is lost through death of spouse, divorce, or marital separation. A jail term, in fourth place, means temporary and sometimes permanent loss of familial, work, and community roles. The fifth, death of a close family member other than the spouse, inevitably leads to the loss of some family role, often parental. Personal injury or illness, in sixth place, may very well lead to loss of roles, although this is not necessarily the case. Fired from a job ranks eighth and retired from work ranks tenth. Interestingly, two positive events are in seventh and ninth places as stress-inducers: getting married and marital reconciliation.

The Holmes Stress Scale

1. Death of spouse	100
2. Divorce	73
3. Marital separation	65
4. Jail term	63
5. Death of close family member	63
6. Personal injury or illness	53

7. Marriage	50
8. Fired at work	47
9. Marital reconciliation	45
10. Retirement	45
11. Change in health of family member	44
12. Pregnancy	40
13. Sex difficulties	39
14. Gain of new family member	39
15. Business readjustment	39
16. Change in financial state	38
17. Death of close friend	37
18. Change to different line of work	36
19. Change in number of arguments with spouse	35
20. Mortgage	31
21. Foreclosure of mortgage or loan	30
22. Change in responsibilities at work	29
23. Son or daughter leaving home	29
24. Trouble with in-laws	29
25. Outstanding personal achievement	28
26. Wife begins or stops work	26
27. Begin or end school	26
28. Change in living conditions	25
29. Revision of personal habits	24
30. Trouble with boss	23
31. Change in work hours or conditions	20
32. Change in residence	20
33. Change in schools	20
34. Change in recreation	19
35. Change in church activities	19
36. Change in social activities	18
37. Mortgage or loan less than $10,000	17
38. Change in sleeping habits	16
39. Change in number of family get togethers	15
40. Change in eating habits	15
41. Vacation	13
42. Christmas	12
43. Minor violations of the law	11

SOURCE: T. H. Holmes and R. H. Rahe, "The Social Readjustment Rating Scale," *Journal of Psychosomatic Research*, 1967, vol. II, pp. 213–218.

A second scale by Barbara S. Dohrenwend and her colleagues ranks 102 life events as to stressfulness. The first five events, in order, are: child died; spouse died; physical illness; went to jail; and divorce. Other events that rank above the average for the 102 items and clearly imply role loss are as follows: in eighth place, convicted of a crime; thirteenth, physical injury; sixteenth, marital separation; twenty-third, close friend died; twenty-fifth, family member other than spouse or child died; thirtieth, business loss or failure; thirty-first, retired; thirty-ninth, moved to a worse residence or neighborhood; and fortieth, fired from job.

In both the Holmes and Dohrenwend scales, loss of the marital role through death or divorce ranks very high. Certainly the spouse may be sorely missed as a person, especially when death terminates the marriage. However, the loss of the marital role is also a highly traumatic event. The research findings in Chapter Five showed that, among men aged thirty-five to forty-four in the United States, the overall death rate is 4.8 times higher for those who are divorced than for those who remain married. The death rate for widowed men of that age is 3.6 times greater than that of the married men. Divorced women of the same age show a death rate 2.2 times that of married women and widowed women one that is 2.6 times the married. Also, one study after another indicates that both widowed and divorced persons have death rates due to coronary heart disease, tuberculosis, cirrhosis of the liver, suicide, and motor vehicle and other accidents that are several times higher than married persons of their age.

As a further illustration, a study by Iwao Marijama and colleagues shows that at *all* ages males and females, white or non-white, who are widowed or divorced have higher death rates from coronary heart disease than their marital counterparts. The following table shows the ratios of death rates from coronary heart disease of the widowed or divorced to those of married persons of the same age. A death ratio of 2.0 for the widowed of a certain age means that their rate is twice that of the married.

Take, for example, white men and women aged thirty-five to forty-four years. The widowed men are 1.8 times more likely to die of coronary heart disease than their married counterparts; the divorced men are 2.5 times more likely. For the women, those who are widowed are 2.3 times more likely to die of coronary heart disease than those who are married; those who are divorced are 2.1 times more likely. Note also that among younger adult white females (aged twenty-five to thirty-four) the rate of death is over five times greater (5.2) for the widowed than for the married.

| | WHITE | | | | NON-WHITE | | | |
| | Male | | Female | | Male | | Female | |
Age	Widowed	Divorced	Widowed	Divorced	Widowed	Divorced	Widowed	Divorced
15-24	1.5	1.8	1.5	1.3	2.1	1.9	1.9	1.4
25-34	2.0	2.8	5.2	2.3	4.2	2.6	2.4	1.3
35-44	1.8	2.5	2.3	2.1	2.6	2.4	2.4	1.4
45-54	1.7	2.2	1.7	1.6	2.7	2.3	2.2	1.4
55-64	1.6	1.9	1.5	1.3	2.2	1.9	2.1	1.4
65-74	1.5	1.7	1.4	1.2	1.8	1.8	1.9	1.4
75-84	1.4	1.6	1.4	1.3	1.6	1.5	1.6	1.3
85 & over	1.4	1.4	1.6	1.4	1.6	1.7	1.9	1.3

Sudden loss or threat of loss of a critical role has a considerable likelihood of leading to sudden death. George Engel analyzed 170 sudden deaths in Rochester, New York. He found that in fifty-nine percent of those death was preceded by these severe losses:

1. After collapse or death of a close person	21.2%
2. During a period of acute grief within the last 16 days	20.6%
3. Threat of loss of a close person	9.4%
4. Loss of status or self-esteem	5.3%
5. Mourning or anniversary of an event	2.9%
	59.4%

Moreover, loss of the marital role is associated with confinement in mental hospitals and jails and prisons. Widowed men are 4.4 times more likely than married men to be hospitalized for mental illness; divorced men are 10.7 times more likely. Widowed women are 1.6 times more likely than women who are married to be mental hospital patients; divorced women are 4.8 times more likely. The figures for incarceration in a correctional institution are, for men, even more striking. Widowed men have a rate of confinement for criminal violations seven times that of married men; divorced men show a rate 17.9 times that of married men. For women, the likelihood of jail or prison is twice as great for the widowed as the married and five times as great for the divorced as the married.

Mental hospitalization and correctional incarceration rates rise markedly, then, when the support of marriage is suddenly removed.

The marital role quite definitely stabilizes individuals. (Single, never married men and women also have higher rates of hospitalization for mental illness than the married.) One explanation for the great rises in rates of conviction and incarceration for crime after widowhood and divorce—especially for men—is this: The disorganization of personality that can result may lead to deviant behavior serious enough to be criminally prosecuted.

James J. Lynch, in *The Broken Heart*, cites a number of studies that indicate a clear link between loss of parents by children and later psychiatric impairment of the children. C. N. Wahl analyzed 392 schizophrenic men, all former navy personnel. Forty percent had lost a parent before age 15 as compared to only 11 percent of the naval men in general. In a second study Roslyn Seligmar and her co-investigators studied 85 adolescents referred for psychiatric evaluation. Early parental loss had been experienced by 36 percent as compared to 12 percent in the adolescent school population generally. Delinquency and school dropout rates in Minnesota were found by Gregory to be significantly higher for children who had lost one or both parents than for other children. J. H. Nolan analyzed psychosis among the Loma of Liberia and found that more than 90 percent had suffered the loss of a parent in childhood.

Lynch also reports on the connection between early loss by children and later physical disease. As one example he points to research by Ralph Poffenburger on 50,000 former students of Harvard and the University of Pennsylvania. Those who later died of coronary heart disease were compared with a control group of healthy former students. Death of either or both parents in childhood was one of the nine major factors that distinguished the diseased from the well.

INVOLUNTARY LOSS OF A JOB

For most of us losing a job is a traumatic event. The stress may be less severe than that for losing a loved one, of course, but it is considerable. Enforced retirement, being fired, being laid off, and giving up a job because of illness are all ways of losing a job one wants to keep. Demotion is another; while the person still has a job it is presumably less desirable than the former one. In the cases of firing and demotion there is the added element of rejection. They are acts that indicate explicitly that a judgment has been made that one either cannot carry out a work role adequately or that one is unwanted in the role for other reasons. The person who loses a work role involuntarily may very well feel a sense of helplessness. Rage toward others is also likely to be felt in the cases of firing and demotion. Self-blame often occurs. There is the sheer changing of behavior routines. There is the void of what to do with the hours previously devoted to work. There is, especially for married men, the sense of failure as a breadwinner, a spouse, and a parent. There is usually severe worry over financial loss. Also, relatedly, there is the fear and the reality of losing status and prestige.

Harvey Brenner carried out a complex analysis of the stressful effects of rising unemployment in the United States in 1970. He found a strong positive correlation between seven measures of stress and unemployment. As unemployment rose so did rates of suicide, admissions to state mental hospitals, admissions to state prisons, criminal homicide, deaths due to cirrhosis of the liver, deaths due to cardiovascular-renal diseases (high blood pressure), and total mortality.

A poignant instance of enforced retirement was documented in *Work in America*, a Report of a Special Task Force to the Secretary of the United States Department of Health, Education and Welfare. A Mr. Winter was sixty-four years old. He loved his job. He conducted a set of complex activities for his company that no one else understood. People left him alone and deferred to him because he did his job so well. On his sixty-fourth birthday he was told that a new young man would work with him for the next year to "learn the tricks of the trade, your trade," as they put it to him. Winter was to train the man who would take over his job upon his retirement at sixty-five.

Winter did not want to retire but the company rules absolutely demanded it. He was apprehensive about training the young man to replace him, but he did his best. The year passed and Winter retired. Immediately he began a psychological and seemingly a physical decline. All zest seeped out of him. He withdrew from life, and spoke to hardly anyone. After a year he was hospitalized and diagnosed as having a senile psychosis. He did not speak to friends or relatives who came to visit him at the hospital. Gradually they stopped coming. Some who knew him well thought he had suffered severe brain damage, although there was no medical substantiation of that.

After Winter had been hospitalized for a year—two years after his retirement—the young man who had replaced him died suddenly. He had been in good health and the company had no one to assume his duties. Company operations slowed to a crawl. No one was able to take over the work because no one understood how to do so. It was a desperate situation. Finally, someone hit upon the idea of asking Winter if he would come back for a few months and train still another person for the job. The man who had this idea did not realize that Winter had been hospitalized. Others who knew of Winter's situation saw no possibility that he could return. Finally, it was decided to approach Winter at the hospital. The situation was desperate; there was nothing to lose.

Four men who had known Winter well on the job went to see him at the hospital. At first he paid them no attention, would not speak, sat there—"a vegetable"—as some had earlier described him. Finally, one of the men got across to Winter the idea that they needed him, wanted him back. He straightened; he spoke a little. Within only a few days he was back on the job, interacting with his co-workers just as he had done before, doing the job as effectively as ever. He was a changed man—changed back to the dynamic and zestful person he had been. However, he had to face the threat of enforced retirement again, of course, as soon as he had trained another.

LOSING UNDESIRED ROLES

It is always prudent to consider carefully whether one really wants to be rid of a role or to substitute one role for another. Certainly it is in many instances, on balance, less stressful and an improvement for a person to be rid of a role. Yet in some instances the loss of a role, even though strongly desired, may turn out to be traumatic. Many a person has sought a divorce or left a job only to suffer disorientation, anxiety, and depression. More often than not the individual is unable to see clearly that the lost role is the source of the problem. Since one elected to be rid of it, one tends not to see the connection between the loss and the present frustration.

Boredom and anger are two of the most common reasons for electing to be rid of a role. One grows tired of a role, often a role that was once altogether interesting. One has learned so well how to carry out the role that it becomes sheer routine. The challenge is no longer there. Or, of course, one may have been bored with a role from the outset—there never was any challenge.

Again, one may be angry because the role demands too much, or too little, or is too restrictive, or has been encroached upon by others. One may vent anger in the process of throwing over a role, and perhaps in throwing over those with whom one interacted in that role. Thus, a spouse is thrown over, or a boss, or co-workers, together with the marital or work situation per se. There may be satisfaction in breaking off the relationship, while the actual role loss becomes a heavy burden.

A major reason special care should be taken in casting off a seemingly undesirable role is that one may well have become dependent on it. Some of us grow to need certain heavy burdens every day at work or at home. Some of us become dependent on a role that, while deadening and boring in itself, balances out the overdemands of another role or vice versa. Some of us have come to need the threat of rejection or encroachment in a role to keep us going in life.

It is also common practice for a person to abandon one role when another role is really the source of stress. Usually this is because the individual feels, rightly or wrongly, that little can be done about the other role. Thus, a married person grows more and more dissatisfied with the spouse and with marriage when the actual source of role dissatisfaction is the job. Little can be done about the job—the person feels that he or she must keep it—and the consequent anger is displaced to the spouse. Or one believes that one is trapped in a marriage and takes action on another front where one feels one has some options: One blames the job and quits. Such mistaken views and misplaced anger almost invariably lead to some degree of stress and misery.

Psychiatrists have long observed that when a problem member of a family suddenly is no longer a problem, one or more other family members may suffer severe stress. The problem member may voluntarily leave or be hospitalized for an extended period. Other family members may at first be consciously quite relieved. Yet some of those members may experience behavioral or health problems.

A common example is the alcoholic husband who disappears or is committed to a hospital. His wife may have suffered because of his erratic and aggressive behavior and because of the lack of funds. Many times she may have wished her husband would leave home or that in some way she could escape the day-in and day-out agony of existence with an alcoholic. Now her wish is a reality. Soon she begins to feel extremely anxious. She does not know what the problem is. She develops painful headaches or other physical symptoms. Just when she feels things have improved, she has become overwrought and ill.

The role changes here are considerable. She cannot cope with them in part because she is not conscious of them as problems. She is unaware that she has become habituated to a role as "the wife of an alcoholic," a role that involves a number of deprivations. She is unaware that her husband's role has cast him as "a problem" and her as "normal," "not a problem." Her role as a "wife of an alcoholic" had been stressful, but she had learned to cope with it. Now that it is gone she has great difficulty coping with the role vacuum that has occurred. This is one reason why couples who fight, whether or not alcohol is involved, so often go back together after a separation. The quarrels and the beatings are less stressful than the void created by the sudden absence of conflicted marital roles.

THE WEEKEND, THE VACATION, AND A SENSE OF LOSS

For many of us, the weekend is a miniature vacation that can be very beneficial. For others, probably an equally large number, it can have stressful consequences. Everyday patterns are disrupted. Even if an occupational role or a housewife role is stressful, there is likely to be regularity to it. One may have worked out a way of adjusting to—coping with—that role that, while not ideal, does reduce stress somewhat. Also, one may have become habituated to a degree of stress in the role so that one needs that stress. Then the weekend may yawn as a void. There may be the sense of too many possible choices to fill it. There may be the letdown that leads to vague feelings of discomforting aimlessness and of depression. Some fill the unknown void with one long round of drinking. Others engage in sexual adventures. Others turn to physical risk—amateur stock car racing, for example. While some welcome the weekend as a brief period of especially rewarding activity and renewal, for all too many it is an unpredictable time to be somehow gotten through, survived—until the predictable routines of the work week can once again be followed.

The vacation of several weeks is culturally labeled as a positive hiatus in the everyday process of living. For some it can be highly rewarding—a combination of a change of pace, a change of scene, and just plain fun. For others things always go wrong: family members get on one another's nerves more than at home or become involved in fights with one another; individuals get involved in accidents or become ill; others suffer a nameless sense of unease; and many are secretly glad when the whole thing is ended and they can get back to their everyday routines.

Certainly the vacation can offer a legitimate escape from a stressful job or other frustrating role conditions. However, the problem is likely to be that one has temporarily lost roles that one depends upon in order to function adequately. If the vacation means leaving behind family, community, and work roles, then so much of one's very being may have been removed that stress mounts rapidly. Since vacations are defined as "good," this is likely to go unrecognized.

Who is one when work and community roles are left behind? Not only are the behavior patterns the person is habituated to suspended. Identity becomes ambiguous. Thus, some people like to vacation each year in a community where they are well known, where others can place them and they can place others. Others combine work and vacation so that the work role goes with them. Still others take on temporary replacement roles, such as hunters, "cowboys," tennis buffs, golfers, and museum goers. The necessity, of course, is to plan a vacation that provides the right mixture of escape from everyday stressful roles and the playing of temporary or permanent roles that provide identity.

UNEXPECTED ROLE LOSS

When one loses a role, the familiar habits for carrying out that role are no longer functional. One may have lost a loved one or a valued job, one may have lost an age role simply by the passage of time, or one may have lost prestige. Apart from the pains of having lost a spouse, income, or status, there is the factor central to all role loss of having no job to go to, no train to catch, no friends to see at work. Much has been written about the good sense of preparing gradually for retirement or for the children growing up and leaving home. But how does one cope with unexpected role loss? How does one cope with the loss of a spouse, a child, a close friend through death or otherwise, or with the loss of a job because of sudden reversal of the company's financial position?

Faced with the fact of role loss, the human tendency is to fight or become depressed. Often to fight is not feasible, and even more often it is inappropriate in the sense that it will be resented by others and in time they will retaliate. Repressing rage and hostility almost inevitably leads to depression. Depression feeds on inaction, lack of involvement; loss of a role means those. Moreover, powerlessness and hopelessness are the handmaidens of depression, and sudden loss often involves a sense of powerlessness and hopelessness. It also means that the old habits are blocked. We are made inactive and uninvolved in that sphere of our lives where the lost role held sway. Thus, a vicious circle of depression and forced disengagement is brought about and perpetuated.

The critical aspect of coping with role loss is to take on—very soon—a suitable substitute role. This may be a temporary or permanent replacement for the lost role. It may be a substitute quite different in some respects from the role that is gone. The word suitable is especially important in this sense: All too often, in the face of role loss, individuals take on other roles that are quite inappropriate and harmful. The wife whose husband suddenly leaves her gets mixed up with "a bad crowd" and finds herself on the edge of a heroin group. Often, here, the individual is seeking high risks as a way of attempting to dispel depression and grief. One must carefully consider the consequences of taking on a new role, of filling the void—even while faced with grief and depression. This is exceedingly difficult to do.

A role should be sought that is challenging and rewarding—one that involves some of the habits of the old role, but that is not directly reminiscent of it. One should try to avoid making a long-term commitment to the new role because, as careful as planning may be, the new role may not work out well. Nevertheless, one should throw oneself into the new role. The aim is to survive the crisis that follows the loss. If it turns out that this replacement role is unduly stressful, it should be abandoned. Alternative roles should be tried. The main point at this stage is involvement.

While working one's way through the trauma of loss—while carrying out this substitute role—long-range plans for replacing the lost role should be made. The current new role may be suitable or it may be best to plan for quite a different role. Almost every change, even an enforced change that involves loss, can be turned to advantage. One may be able to form more rewarding and enduring relationships than before. One may be able to turn a work career in a decidedly more satisfying direction. Life is change. Loss is a form of change; so is self-renewal.

12

New Roles

THE LACK OF PREPARATION

We move through life shedding old roles and taking on new ones. A person's social life is a process of role change. Realistically, we should, then, welcome taking on new roles in the family, at work, or in the community. We should also realistically guard against undue stress in doing so. Yet we tend to cling to the old, familiar roles and close our eyes to impending role change.

As a result, in assuming a new role it is often the unknown factors that cause stress. What are the expectations for the role? How is the role to be carried out? Will one be able to perform adequately? One may know what behaviors are required and yet be very unclear about what actually to do to achieve the behavioral results. Knowing what is expected and doing it are two different things.

The reason stress results from unknown factors in assuming a role is, of course, that we are fearful of failure and of the disapproval and other penalties that may result. The less prepared we are for a new role, the greater the stress. The more central to our lives the role is, the greater the stress; family and work roles are often more critical to us than others. When we take on an undesirable role, even though we have little choice in the matter, we may well feel much stress. This is not only because it is frustrating in itself to assume a role we do not want. It is also because, through past learning, we are likely to be conditioned to seek reward for carrying out a role adequately, *any* role, and to avoid punishment for poor role performance.

It is striking how few systematic procedures there are in our society for learning many roles. About the only training for the marital and parental roles is whatever one observed years earlier as to how one's parents carried out the roles. There are, to be sure, many educational and training programs designed to prepare one for certain aspects of numerous job roles. That is, they provide knowledge about the techniques required, but they seldom provide realistic conditions for putting those techniques into practice.

Of course, people do learn family, work, and other roles in some fashion or other. However, the process is too often hit-or-miss and so gives rise to anxiety about whether one can handle the role. Study, planning, and practice for taking on a role are only sensible. However, the mere mention of that occasions mild ridicule in many contexts. It is acceptable, even required, that one learn professional work roles ahead of time in that fashion: doctor, lawyer, architect, and so on. They are the exceptions; but study, planning, practice to be a wife or husband, mother or father, middle-aged person?

MEASURING STRESS IN NEW ROLES

The two scales discussed in Chapter Eleven indicate the relative stressfulness of various changes in life conditions, many of which centrally involve taking on new roles or shedding old ones. The most stressful role changes are those involving loss of family roles due to deaths of spouses and of sons and daughters and to divorce. However, the taking on of other roles, including those generally held to be desirable, can also have high stress loadings.

The first of the two scales, developed by Thomas H. Holmes, ranks forty-three stressful events and assigns impact weights to each: the higher the impact score the greater the stress. One hundred is the maximum score and zero the minimum. Of the role changes that most individuals would define as desirable, the four most stressful are: marriage, with an impact score of fifty; marital reconciliation, forty-five; gain of new family member, thirty-nine; and outstanding personal achievement, twenty-eight.

The second scale, by Barbara S. Dohrenwend, a sociologist, and her colleagues, ranks 102 life events as to stressfulness but does not assign specific weights. The most stressful changes that involve the taking on of roles usually evaluated positively or as improvement in roles are:

Rank
6. Birth of a first child
14. Marital couple reunited after separation
18. Relations with spouse changed for the better
22. Married
26. Birth of a second or later child
27. Adopted a child
28. Built a home
33. Started a business or profession
35. Expanded business or profession
36. Had financial improvement unrelated to work
46. Changed jobs for a better one
47. Moved to a better residence or neighborhood
50. Promoted in job

Moving, changing residence and community, inevitably means losing old community roles and taking on new ones. For the young it may mean changing school roles. For adults it often, although not always, means taking on a new job role. Individuals who move within a country or from one country to another have been shown by one study after another to have more behavioral and health problems than other people.

Although there are difficulties in measurement, most analyses show a death rate that is about 5 percent higher for white males in the United States who are foreign-born than for those who are native-born. The figure is 19 percent for females. Death rates from accidents of all kinds are almost twice as high for foreign-born as for native-born whites. The rate for native-born is 47 per 100,000 and for foreign-born, 83 per 100,000.

We are a highly mobile society. From 1970 to 1974, 43 percent of the families in the United States changed residence. Coronary heart disease is distinctly more common among those who are mobile within the United States than among those who are not. Lung cancer rates are higher for those who migrate to cities in the United States than for those who were born in the cities.

Rates of suicide and mental disorders are distinctly higher for those who change residence often than for those who do not. Whenever poor people move in the United States, rates of emotional disturbances increase. This is true even when they move to what they consider to be better neighborhoods.

The families of managers and administrators are especially stressed by moving from one community to another. And it is part of the manager's way of life that in the United States he and his family move often. Of managers aged twenty-five to forty years, 68 percent move at least once every three years; 23 percent move every two years; and 18 percent move once a year or more often. Most of these moves are within the same organization or to a similar organization; some, of course, represent the taking on of a distinctly new work role. But it is often the wives and children of the corporate nomads who suffer the greatest stress. The husband-father carries with him his role identity as a manager. The children have to give up school and friendship roles and take on new ones. Wives cannot carry their community roles with them as their husbands can often carry their work roles. The wife who has built up a role as a competent person in the community must give that up, lose the status that goes with it. She must, in a sense, start at the bottom in the new community, create a sense of acceptance and esteem all over again. The abrupt shifting of roles creates social discontinuity and instability, especially for wives and children. This, in turn, is likely to lead to conflict between their roles and the husband-father roles.

MARITAL AND PARENTAL ROLES

Recruitment criteria and procedures vary greatly from one type of role to another. To enter many professional and technical occupations one must satisfy numerous, involved criteria as to personal characteristics and training. These serve to maintain standards of performance. They also serve sometimes to maintain the image and prestige of the occupation. How many ugly, dishevelled doctors does one see? Their looks have little to do with their abilities. Regardless of what medical schools may say, applicants who make a poor appearance are usually weeded out, denied admission. The dignified, prestigious image of the profession is maintained.

In contrast, just about anyone can get married and raise a family. True, to limit who can do so has serious implications as to individual freedom. However, raising children is as fundamentally important as any work in the society, and there are virtually no criteria that must be met in order to do so, including ones of preparation and training.

Marriage is not an especially stressful event in all societies. In many the responsibilities of husband and wife are clearly understood ahead of time, they do not conflict appreciably, and there are opportunities for practicing beforehand. Not so in the United States and numerous other western, "advanced" societies. Getting married means the shock of taking on myriad little understood responsibilities. Above all, it means having to live closely with someone else, carrying on an intimate relationship day-in and day-out, and either meshing one's needs and actions with those of the marital partner or suffering high levels of conflict, anguish, disappointment, and stress. Most, if not all, of the major pressures of living in modern society come to bear on marriage. Marriage is the role relationship that can be most effective in coping with the stresses of the job, of being parents, or of other roles. Two people, husband and wife, working closely and effectively together, can be a formidable team. Alternately, marriage can be the role relationship where the stresses and strains of life find aggressive outlets. This is a major reason why, in a minority of marriages, husband-wife violence is rampant.

Murray A. Straus, a leading researcher on family violence, conducted a national study of violence between husbands and wives and parents and their children. He found that severe violence—that is, serious assault—occurred at least once within a given year in 6.1 percent of married couples. Wives were violent slightly more often than husbands: In 4.6 percent of the couples wives assaulted husbands, while in 3.8 percent husbands assaulted wives. Parents seriously assaulted a given child over the year in 4.0 percent of the families; a given child assaulted one or both parents during the year in 9.4 percent of the families.

Careful preparation for marriage, now lacking, can go far not only toward reducing violence between spouses. It can do much to set the stage for making marriage the most rewarding as well as the most enduring of human relationships. Preparation for the parental role is almost as inadequate as that for the marital role. There are numerous books on child rearing, but that is about all that is available for the average person. Those books vary greatly; many conflict with each other. In any case, most tell how to train a child as if that were something that is done to or for the child rather than the consequence of a parent-child role relationship. Almost everyone has been "brought up" by parents or surrogate parents. How they acted as parents no doubt affects considerably how we act with our children. Even though we remember little of the early years, we very likely style our parental behavior after that of our parents. In some cases we may act in quite opposite ways, as a response to frustrating relationships with our parents years ago. Unless we have brothers or sisters who are much younger than we are, we have had no opportunity to observe directly how they carried out the parental roles in relation to young children.

Even brief consideration leads one to realize that being a parent is an awesome responsibility. The central aims of the parental role are to care for the basic needs of offspring and to help them become psychologically and physically healthy, constructive, contributing members of the society. In good part this involves helping the young to learn how to take on and carry out roles adequately. It also involves helping them to cope with role stress and to avoid being strait jacketed by role demands. The responsibilities of being a parent are seldom cast in terms of helping children to become role players. Yet that is much of what parents do, for better or for worse.

Above all, parents are teachers. Teaching involves helping students to learn about the world, to learn how to cope with the world, and to learn how to change the world. Teachers are guides to a future they themselves have never seen. They rely on knowledge and experience to act as guides, usually to the young. This is what parents do or try to do or should try to do, as the case may be. Yet they have so very little training for this. No one is teaching the teachers. In some so-called "primitive" societies, children grow up in extended families. Here young girls may have ample opportunity to observe relatives raising their children. Very likely they help out in the rearing of the children of aunts and uncles, older cousins, and of their own younger siblings. In "modern" societies little of this obtains in the nuclear family setting.

There are hopeful signs. Some mothers and fathers make conscious efforts to learn about being parents. Fathers, as well as mothers, may arrange to spend ample time with their young children. There are community "cope" groups of expectant mothers and of young parents. However, it is time, far past time, that we made conscious societal-wide plans to improve conditions for learning to be a parent. We should seek to change those attitudes that hold that formal, institutionalized arrangements for training to be a parent are to be avoided. There is a prevailing view that such arrangements connote self-conscious attempts to do the impossible. Some training is very likely to be better than none. It is in part the awesomeness of the tasks of being a parent that impedes us from learning the role. If we do not have opportunities to prepare for the role, then we are more able to avoid blaming ourselves when we fail at it. That is one of the unspoken mechanisms that perpetuates our flagrantly haphazard approach to becoming parents.

PROBLEMS OF SUCCESS

How many people have wished over and over to have all the money they need? A couple goes along, year-in and year-out, trying to make ends meet. He is a repairman at a hotel. She works part time as a maid there. They have two children, one of whom is nearing college age and wants to study veterinary medicine. The parents see no way of paying the college costs. Suddenly they win $100,000 a year for life in the state lottery. They are besieged by newsmen. They are on television. They will spend the money wisely, they say. A new car? Well, yes, but a Ford; nothing extravagant. He will leave his job? "I'll take a little vacation," he responds, "then we'll see." Will his wife work? No, she will stay home and take care of the house. What else? Well, they would like to take a trip. Where? The Bahamas, maybe—they've always dreamed of going there. But that will be their only extravagance. What do the men and women they work with at the hotel think? "They took us to lunch the other day," he says. "Eighteen of them. We paid." He laughs. "We had a good time. No change," he says firmly. "They know we don't change just because of—of being lucky."

In case after case of this type, a few years later the lucky couple wishes they had never been lucky. If they keep on in their jobs, their co-workers grow to resent working alongside someone who does not have to work. Their friends feel uncomfortable with someone who "has money." If they go out to dinner with friends and do not pay the bill they are thought to be cheap. If they do pay they are thought to be patronizing. Usually, their sudden monetary gain has not been accompanied by an upward shift in prestige roles. They do not have friends of higher prestige and their old friends are uncomfortable with them. If they do not work, they have little to do. If they do work, they are resented on the job. They cannot handle the unexpected, although initially desirable, role changes. They are often miserable.

Other persons have sudden occupational success either at a young age or after years of struggle: the author whose first novel is a best seller; the author whose first six novels sold poorly but whose seventh is a runaway hit; or the singer or actor who has comparable success. Some cope with the consequent life changes very well. Others cannot cope. Some drink excessively or use other harmful drugs, some become depressed and morose, and a few commit suicide.

Why are some individuals unable to cope with success roles for which they have striven long and hard? They have become so habituated to the stress of striving that success is a terrible letdown. It means severe decompression. They have lost the role of struggling underdog. The new success roles often present too little challenge in themselves. They fear the void that seems to yawn ahead. At the same time, they fear losing the success role that means so much in terms of prestige.

In addition, success in a work role often demands taking on other roles. One is likely to take on a social class role of higher prestige. One may be expected to carry out community leadership roles for which one is ill-prepared. Inevitably, there are expectations that one will take on new friendship roles. Individuals sometimes resolve the whole stressful situation by self-destructive behavior—for example, excessive drinking—that causes them to lose the roles so hard won. They are back to the striver role. Sometimes they eventually succeed again and repeat the whole cycle.

TAKING ON NEW ROLES

It seems only reasonable that individuals would prepare carefully to take on important roles. Except for certain occupational roles, however, this is seldom done. As discussed earlier, to plan in detail how to take on a marital role, a parental role, a friendship role, and many community and other roles smacks in many quarters of calculation—a certain brand of insincerity, a derogatory absence of spontaneity. We are expected to do "naturally" that which we actually do well only by foresight and practice.

The first necessity in planning to take on a new role is to determine what the expectations for the role are. These may be formalized and written down. They may be informal and available only by talking to and observing others. In any case, in taking on a new role one would be well advised to find out all one reasonably can about what is expected of persons who hold that role. What are they expected to do and how are they expected to do it? What and how are two different, if closely related, matters. Knowing what to do as a parent of a newborn child and doing it are hardly the same.

The individual can learn how to do what is required in a given role in a number of ways. There may or may not be written instructions available. There may or may not be educational or training programs available. One may be able to observe others carrying out the role and use them as models. One may be able to practice the role before actually taking it on. One may be able to intern or apprentice in the role.

Understanding, at least to some degree, the nature of the roles of other persons in relation to the role one is taking on is a further necessity. Roles are not carried out in social vacuums. They are enacted in relation to roles carried out by other persons. Thus, some grasp of those other roles is essential to success in a given role.

At an early point in the process of taking on a role, it is important for a person to determine, if at all possible, whether he or she has the abilities necessary to carry out the role. Does one have the sheer technical competence? If not, can one gain it? Does one have a style of role playing that is suitable or will the style always be at odds with the role? Sometimes, of course, we have little choice. Age roles, for example, lie ahead and we must do the best we can to carry them out.

It is equally important for the person to determine what the stresses of the role and whether he or she can adequately cope with them. Will the role conflict severely with other roles that one must carry out? Will it bring one into serious role conflict with other persons? Are the demands of the new role, in relation to one's abilities and emotional makeup, too great to be tolerable? Alternately, is the role so undemanding as to be intolerable? Again, is the role unduly restrictive of one's need for self-expression? What is the likelihood of rejection in the role? What is the likelihood of encroachment by others?

Determination of stress is addressed in later chapters of this book. However, it is important for the individual contemplating a new role to appraise realistically its stresses or frustrations and its rewards as well. Too often individuals needlessly take on new roles that for any of many reasons are exceedingly stressful. Going "from the frying pan to the fire" is frequently easy. Reversing the process, once the leap to the new role is made, may be very difficult and in some instances impossible.

If one is to go ahead in the taking on of a new role, what—in addition to knowledge about the role, observation of role models, and practice in the role—is required? It is well to monitor one's progress in carrying out the role. Is one able, gradually, to learn the necessary behaviors and attitudes? If so, is this done without unduly debilitating stressful effects? Is there a point of no return after which one cannot turn back, relinquish the role? Has that point been reached? If not, when will it be? What are the criteria for success in the role? Meeting minimal expectations is one thing; carrying out a role so that one gains the rewards of clear success is often another. Observation and study of those who have been especially successful in the role can be of great benefit. As noted earlier, all this may connote a degree of distasteful calculation. Perhaps it does. Yet, the roles we play are central to our lives and our well-being. Learning roles adequately, carrying out roles well, and finding reward rather than frustration in doing so are all matters too important to be left to the conventional wisdom.

13

Role Rejection and Encroachment

FORMS OF REJECTION

Role rejection involves being forced out of a role one already has or being blocked from attempting to gain a role. Common examples of the first are: one spouse being rejected by the other with separation or divorce the result; rejection of a lover; permanent rejection of a child by a parent ("You are no child of mine"); rejection of a parent by a son or daughter; a student who is dismissed from school; or a worker who is fired or in some instances retired.

In the second category of rejection, blockage from attaining a role, some usual instances are these: a proposal of marriage that is rebuffed; a student who is denied admission to college; another who is not promoted in school; a job applicant who is turned away; or a worker who is turned down for promotion to a more responsible job.

Rejection may come because others judge that one has performed poorly or will do so in a new role. Other reasons are because there are too many aspirants to a role, because others use rejection as a form of aggression, or because others simply do not want a person in a given situation, although he or she is technically qualified. Whatever the reason, rejection is likely to be a painful experience and is likely to lead to stress. This can be so even when the role is not one we especially value.

In a highly competitive society like the United States, role rejection is widespread and a major source of stress. Extreme competition for success goals of money, prestige, and power means severe competition on the job. Thus, many lose out in the economic race and in one way or another suffer role rejection. This, in turn, means that competition for the education necessary to get the job that may lead to the success goals is also severe. As a consequence, rejection is also common here. Moreover, rejection in the economic sphere often leads to aggression within the family. Anger over rejection is displaced to spouses or to offspring. They, in turn, become aggressive and the end result may be separation, divorce, or run away children.

AVOIDING AND SEEKING REJECTION

We are exceedingly vulnerable to evaluations by others as unsuitable for a role either when we aspire to it or after we begin to carry it out. We are all, of necessity, role players. We know intuitively, unconsciously, that roles are the social mechanisms by which we draw support from the environment and in large measure relate to each other. We have also learned, by hard experience, that role rejection means psychological rejection—withdrawal of warmth and approval and the replacement of those with coldness and disapproval. Rejection, either before or after taking on a role, is a threat to our well-being.

Thus, some of us grow fearful of attempting to take on new roles. The pain of past rejections and failures may lead us to go to great lengths to avoid risking any further rejection. Yet, new roles must be taken on. As a result, many persons find the assuming of new age roles, new job roles, new family roles, and new community roles (after a change in residence), an exceedingly stressful, nearly intolerable burden.

Others of us actually seek out role rejection compulsively. While this is often viewed as strange behavior, it is not especially uncommon. People develop this pattern mainly for several related reasons. Those who have been rejected time and again no longer want to risk the disappointment of being rejected. Yet they have survived one rejection after another, and so rejection has become associated with, in a sense has come to stand for, survival. Bringing on rejection of oneself by others means that individual takes control of matters. One will not be disappointed if, from the outset, rejection is certain. At the same time, the individual has the sense of once again surviving in a hostile world. Those who actively bring on rejection time after time are seldom aware of their own motivations. They tend to think they are dogged by bad luck and malevolent others.

A CASE OF AGGRESSION IN RESPONSE TO REJECTION

As with the other sources of role stress, responses run the gamut from aggression toward others to self-blame and self-aggression, to distortion of reality, to extreme withdrawal, and to risk taking in the hope of reversing impending or actual rejection. The case of a twenty-eight year old mother illustrates the extremes to which responses to rejection can lead. It was raining and she was hanging washed clothes in the basement to dry. Her son, aged three, came down the basement stairs, followed by a neighbor's child of the same age. The woman grabbed the neighbor's boy by the ankles, swung him around several times, crashing his head against a metal post that held up the floor above. The child died soon after. The woman sank to the floor and remained in a trance-like state for weeks.

In a state mental hospital, the woman was placed in a deep hypnotic state. She told of her desire to be accepted in the neighborhood where she lived. She and her husband had moved there two years previously. At first, other couples invited them to parties. Then all invitations stopped. It was an upper middle class community where mainly young professional couples lived. The woman's husband was a truck driver. He had not graduated from high school; neither had she. After finding that they were not college graduates, did not speak or dress well, and that the husband drove a truck, the neighbors avoided them.

Under hypnosis, this woman told of her early life of poverty in an ethnic enclave, of her desire to get out and to be successful. Her father had been a sadistic man who lost job after job. He had beaten her and her mother badly many times. She left high school, ran away from home, and finally got a job as a waitress in a truck stop restaurant. There she met her husband. After marriage she continued to work as a waitress. Her husband drove the truck for eighty hours a week. They lived in a run down tenement. For seven years they saved every penny they possibly could in order to buy a house in a good neighborhood. Now they were clearly rejected there. She spoke, under hypnosis, of her consequent anger. She especially blamed the mother of the little boy whom she had killed. She saw her as the ring leader of those who rejected her. She retaliated by an extreme version of the behavior that her father had used.

A CASE OF REJECTION
FOR PROMOTION

John S. had worked at a savings bank in a large city for twenty-four years—since graduating from college. He had been a vice-president for four years and was about to be named executive vice-president. Suddenly, the picture changed. The bank president, called G. R. here, came to the point: Allegations had been made about John's personal life and that was holding up his appointment as executive vice-president. What allegations, John demanded to know. G. R. answered that the allegations were not about John exactly. Rather, they were about his wife. John was bewildered and angry. There were rumors that John's wife had had affairs with several men recently, one of whom was employed at the bank, G. R. said.

Those rumors were completely untrue, John said. G. R. said he agreed, but that what bothered the board of directors was that so many people appeared to believe them. The bank's reputation was spotless, G. R. went on, and of course the bank could not afford to have even a hint of scandal.

John had grown extremely agitated. Good God, did the bank ruin people's careers on the basis of some totally unfounded rumors? Suddenly John set forth an explanation. The rumors had been spread by one of the other vice-presidents who had also wanted the promotion to executive vice-president. The board had thought of that, G. R. said, and had checked out each of them. No, they had no part in spreading any rumors. G. R. went on to say that the appointment of an executive vice-president would be held up for several months. Perhaps the rumors would fade away.

But the rumors persisted and three months later another man was appointed to the position. John felt trapped. He had never discussed the rumors with his wife. He knew it would upset her terribly. He just told her he had been passed over. He did not talk about the matter with others for fear of spreading the rumors even further in the process. Gradually, John became withdrawn and morose. He did his work but he was uncommunicative. He was moved to a less visible part of the bank floor. He had a recurring thought that there was a plot afoot to push him out of the bank. He became uncommunicative with his wife as well. He began to think that the rumors about her might be true. He hired a private detective to monitor her activities.

John began to make mistakes in his work, sometimes serious ones. He started to drink heavily. The president, G. R., became aware of John's mistakes and surmised that he had a drinking problem. John was assigned an assistant, which he had never had before. Gradually the young assistant came to do most of John's work. John resented him, but he was also relieved that someone took some of his workload. John continued to drink heavily. He started questioning his wife about her daily activities. She became alarmed. Finally, she told him she thought he should see a psychiatrist. He became violently angry, then withdrawn. For several weeks they did not speak.

G. R. discussed John's case with the members of the bank's board of directors. All agreed that he had to go. Whatever the reason, the bank could not have a senior officer who projected a hostile image—and a drunk on top of that. It was certainly a good thing John had not been promoted to executive vice-president, G. R. told the board members. John had been with the bank twenty-five years. They decided to offer him retirement at half his present pay. He could take it or leave it, they agreed.

John was informed by letter of the board's decision. First, he refused. Then he accepted. He had no choice. By now he believed the earlier rumors about his wife, although others had forgotten them. He separated from her. He continued to drink heavily. He had been given thirty days notice at the bank. On his last day, he did not appear. There was to be a farewell party for him that Friday afternoon. At nine-thirty that morning he shot himself in the head. The wound was not fatal. He was hospitalized. He sank into a deep depression. When the wound had healed, he was moved to a mental hospital. It was all due to the fact that he had a drinking problem, people said.

THE NATURE OF ROLE ENCROACHMENT

We often become greatly committed to our roles. They become part of us. They are our possessions. Just as animals feel threatened by encroachment of others on their physical territory, we are threatened by encroachment of others on our social territory—our roles. When someone attempts to take over any of the rights and duties in one or another of our roles, we are likely to see that as an attack upon us. Successful encroachment by others ultimately means loss of all or part of a role. Actual or presumed role encroachment is a major source of antagonism and ill feeling between people.

Role encroachment is the source of much friction in the family, especially between in-laws and between one generation and another. The wife-mother may experience severe annoyance when her mother-in-law, or her own mother, attempts to take over the running of the home and the guidance of the children. The husband-father may become incensed when the son-in-law gives him financial advice and tips on how to get ahead in his job. Again, the grandmother may seem to try to take over her daughter's wife and mother roles or the grandfather his son's husband and father roles.

Role encroachment is equally common in the work situation. The corporate vice-president is likely to fight with tooth and nail if someone tries to move in on his "territory," meaning his rights and responsibilities. When the "new member of the club"—the new worker in the office, for example—tries to tell the old timers how to do this or that, he or she is likely to be squelched very quickly. That, too, is role encroachment.

The foreman always sits at a particular location at the long dining table at lunch time. If a new worker pre-empts his place, there can be trouble. In many organizations, the material symbols a person displays are not to duplicate those of higher rank. The junior executive who drives the same type of car as a senior executive may be thought to be too big for his britches. The bank teller who dresses like a bank president may be thought to be overdoing it.

Of course, role encroachment is also a tactic often used to "freeze" someone out in business or other situations. The executive's duties and responsibilities are gradually stripped away by his superiors, soon leaving little but the title, in an effort to force him to resign. The title may be even upgraded, while authority and responsibility are downgraded.

Children show the same tendencies. This is part of the reason that the four-year-old may resent the new baby in the family so greatly. It is why the ten-year-old captain of the little league baseball team will tolerate no one usurping his leadership role.

Why is it that there is derision and resentment directed against the older person who tries to act or dress younger than his or her age? Part of the answer lies in role encroachment. The young resent any attempt to make them seem old and foolish, and the old resent attempts on the parts of those their age to indicate that their age role is not desirable. Why is it that there is such a strong negative reaction to those of one sex who act and dress like those of the other? In part because of role encroachment. Such behavior is seen as an attempt to subvert the sex role.

The fact that we sometimes joke about role encroachment, often a little nervously, belies our underlying concern. When it happens to someone else, it can be highly humorous. Seldom is this so when it happens to us. It is fair to say that, in many respects, we are very tough beings. Yet, social psychologically, we are very fragile and vulnerable. Small threats to our roles and to our place in society often upset us greatly—cause much stress and anger. This is why some oriental societies place such great emphasis on "saving face."

III

COPING WITH ROLE STRESS

14

The Coping Process

INTRODUCTION

There is a great deal that individuals can do to cope effectively with role stress. Persistence, flexibility, and innovation are required. So is a perspective that recognizes role stress as a real and significant source of problems in most people's lives. However, that perspective must include the recognition that it is altogether possible either to change or to modify social roles.

Too many individuals pay little attention to their roles—in fact, they deny their existence. We in the United States take essentially a psychological view of life, that individuals behave as they do because of inner needs to adjust to the world around them. Of those who do recognize the great influence of roles in our lives, many are likely to feel despair. Roles are so powerful and pervasive, they believe, that it is all but impossible to do anything about them. This is not true, but if people believe it to be so, then—for practical purposes—it has the effect of being true and so impedes effective coping.

It is important to understand that a psychological view of life almost inevitably leads to the conclusion that if one has problems the solution lies in *adjusting* to them, in some way rearranging oneself and modifying one's behavior to fit better with the world around one. There is very little, if any, emphasis on changing the surrounding environment. To be sure, there are schools of psychology that do emphasize change outside of oneself; they are not, however, at all in the mainstream of popular thinking. In any case, coping effectively with role stress is not simply a matter of inner psychological adjustment. That is often important and necessary. So is reallocating interpersonal and natural resources so that they are more effectively utilized to cope with role stress. However, effective coping will also usually involve changing the social environment, which is to say the network of role relationships in which one lives. Bending and warping oneself to fit into stressful roles is really quite destructive of the self. Engaging in innovative behavior that changes one's social environment is rewarding both because one is getting at the source of the problem and because one feels a sense of creative coping, of achievement, and of liberation.

Coping effectively with a role stress problem will, then, often involve—in varying degrees—bringing about change in one's roles, change in one's ways of perceiving and behaving, and reallocation of one's resources. The point to be made at this juncture is that bringing about change in one's roles is a critical part of the process of coping with role stress and one that is seldom carried out in a planned and rational way.

RESOURCE ALLOCATION

The individual's central resources in coping with role stress are the ability to innovate and to learn effective coping behaviors. Money, influence, and power are, of course, important—but they do not automatically resolve or alleviate stress problems. If they did, there would be far fewer powerful, wealthy people who suffer the consequences of severe role stress. Friends obviously are a potent resource in dealing with stress. It is mainly because of the roles we hold that we have the friends we do. In any case, friends are excellent sounding boards for discussing plans for changing one's roles. Many are especially good at suggesting solutions to problems for others if not for themselves. Some can provide the right kind of influence at the right time in the right place. Still others are simply not able to be of any direct help in coping with stress; by being there, however, they may provide important moral support.

When individuals analyze how they are allocating their resources in regard to the roles they carry out, they are frequently greatly surprised. They often find that their psychological and other resources are being squandered on nonessentials. One major reason is that individuals are prone to deny the existence of a role problem, to hope it will simply go away. To bring resources to bear, one must recognize the existence of the problem and the need to cope with it.

Then, too, individuals often focus their resources on roles where there are few problems. There is a sense of achievement there. Resources are overused in the hope of more and more success. For example, a husband may put great amounts of time and energy into his family roles, where relationships are very positive. He may increasingly slight his job to do so. Then, if he is laid off or fired, he is likely to suffer depression as well as the severe problem of not having an income with which to support his family. A close-knit, loving family is a very positive part of life. However, it simply is not a substitute for a job and income. For most people the two, family and job, are not interchangeable.

Resources are always limited. They need to be allocated carefully. Individuals need to see clearly what their role stress problems are and to recognize explicitly what resources they possess and how these resources can best be employed in coping with stress. Use of the Role Stress Inventory, discussed in the next chapter, is a tangible aid toward that end.

CHANGING ATTITUDES AND BEHAVIOR

As indicated earlier, the extreme emphasis on adjustment by the individual to the environment that the psychological society advocates can be harmful. The individual is expected to cope and to change the self in ways that he or she cannot, to conform to impossible demands. This kind of one-way adjustment—self-change in the individual without change in the surrounding social environment—seldom draws on the innovative, expressive capacities of the person. Thus, attempts to conform and to measure up in stressful role situations are very likely to engender more stress.

Nevertheless, there is one broad area where a person can often effect some constructive self-change. This has to do with one's attitudes toward, and perceptions of, role demands. The individual can learn to see that failure to meet role demands usually will not have dire consequences. In some instances, to be sure, that may very well be so, but much of the time a degree of slippage in meeting demands is tolerated by others. The problem here is that many people have learned, through certain specific traumatic experiences, that failure to meet role demands can lead to severe punishment, and they may generalize that to all role demands.

The necessity is to distinguish between role demands that really should be met in order to insure the welfare of oneself and others and those that need not necessarily be met. Looked at one way, social life is a matter of priorities, of deciding which role demands take priority over others. In some situations it is prudent to explain beforehand to those who may be affected that one will not be able to meet certain role demands. Sometimes an explanation after the fact is useful. Often no explanation at all is necessary, since others will not be adversely affected.

In any case, it is well for individuals to see that in most instances role expectations have developed often over many, many years for *all* holders of a given role. They do not, as a rule, take individual differences into account. If one tries to meet all the expectations of one's roles at a given time, one may, as on a never ending treadmill, end up exhausted—stressed beyond endurance. If one orders one's role expectations into priorities, and if failure to meet those of lower priority leads to problems, then those lower priority roles may need to be shed or otherwise changed. Generally, however, judicious selection of role demands to be met will suffice and there will be little negative consequences when others are not met.

Then, too, individuals may make demands on one that are not appropriate to the role. Personal desires are substituted for legitimate role expectations. The boss wants the worker to do some personal service for him that does not bear on the job. One spouse insists that the other share his or her political views. More often another person simply makes demands that *extend* the role expectations upon the given individual. In but one type of example, the telephone may be the instrument. The student studying for an examination calls the teacher for help on Sunday morning. The person with a minor illness calls the physician at three in the morning. The housewife insists that the police department send an officer to fix a leaking faucet or to rescue her cat from a tree.

Individuals can learn to reject quixotic and unreasonable personal demands upon them made under the pretext of legitimate role demands. One can also elect not to meet legitimate role demands of low priority. Understanding the nature of one's roles—the differences between critical and unimportant demands and between legitimate and illegitimate demands—is a necessity if this is to be effectively done.

INNOVATION

Innovation is the process of creating new solutions to problems of any kind. This usually involves putting together two or more already existing ideas or material things in a new way so that a problem is solved. Material things may or may not be involved. A man recently flew across the English Channel under his own power. For decades there have been attempts to create an aircraft propelled by human power that would actually fly beyond a few feet; all failed. This man essentially took a bicycle and a glider and put them together so that they would work.

In England someone had the idea of putting together—pairing— psychotic women without children and orphaned, withdrawn children. The idea worked. They were able to communicate with and to support each other. In this country, the director of a small mental hospital had the idea of taking his patients, many of whom had violent tendencies, to a summer resort for a vacation. While there the patients acted like guests at a resort hotel, not like individuals with severe mental problems.

A medical school student was blinded in an accident just before receiving his M.D. degree. His dreams of becoming a surgeon were shattered. He went to a psychiatrist for help. During one of the sessions, the idea occurred to him: Be a psychiatrist. That was one medical role he could carry out well without sight.

A woman with four small children wanted desperately to get out of the house, get a job. There was no one to take care of the children, no place to take them. She started a day care center. Soon she had assistants and was starting other centers in other communities. That is true role innovation.

A man with a social work degree was in charge of diagnosing new inmates at a prison. He made careful attempts to diagnose why the new inmates had committed crimes. His diagnoses were ignored by the warden and the staff. He grew to hate his job. Suddenly his wife was stricken with polio. Upon her return from the hospital, there was no one to look after her. He could not leave the prison during working hours to do so. Then the idea occurred to him: Become a parole officer. He did so. Now he was free to set his own hours. He was able to put his diagnoses into action, and he was able to look after his wife.

Coping with role stress problems means innovating changes in one's roles—either modifying or adding or dropping one or more roles. Necessity is the mother of innovation. Naturally. When there is no problem, there is no need for a solution. However, solutions are seldom arrived at when people are under severe stress. Stress makes us tighten up, become rigid and inflexible. The conditions needed for innovation are quite the opposite: what is needed is flexibility of thought. Moreover, solutions to problems often "just come" to one, out of the blue. However, if we just wait for solutions to come, we *could* wait forever.

In any case, study after study shows that the conditions that further creative insight and problem solving in general can be brought about by most people. First of all, assemble as much information as possible about the problem. If the problem one is trying to solve is personal, get away from it temporarily. Then diagnose what is causing the problem. Let the mind free-wheel as to possible solutions. Set aside trying to solve the problem and go back to the everyday routine. A few days or even hours later get some distance from the problem once again, review the possible solutions on the list, and devise others. Choose the most likely solution and try it out on an experimental basis. Monitor the results, modify the proposed solution as necessary, and continue with it—or replace it with another that now seems most likely to be effective. Then, evaluate progress and decide when the problem is resolved.

This is the problem-solving process. It applies to problems in all phases of life—in the home or in the scientist's laboratory. Yet, in regard to role stress and other problems of everyday life, we seldom use it. We may say: It would not work for me; there is just no solution to my problem. We may be self-conscious about using this problem-solving process. These blockages to problem solving in everyday life develop partly because we simply are not used to, not in the habit of, following the steps just outlined.

A person is beset by some particular family or work problems or a combination of the two. He or she does not know which way to turn. Then someone says, "Collect as much information as possible about the problem, get away from the problem, go to some quiet place, and let your mind free-wheel over possible solutions." The person may well conclude that such advice is outlandish. Here a person is faced with a horrendous, seemingly insolvable problem and someone is telling that person to collect information about it and take a little vacation.

What is really abortive is remaining in the role stress situation day-in and day-out and doing what one has been doing. In some cases, of course, it may be that in a short time the problem will resolve itself and one is best advised to just wait it out. More often, however, continuing as usual will only lead to greater and greater stress and negative consequences.

Once a person starts the problem-solving process there is the feeling that finally one is doing something active about the problem, finally one has taken at least indirect control of the situation—although even a tentative solution has not yet been reached. This will help one to keep moving on a problem-solving path.

15

The Role Stress Inventory

THE INVENTORY

The Role Stress Inventory is divided into three parts.* The first enables individuals to pinpoint which of their roles are giving rise to stress; it also locates the sources of stress as conflict, overdemand, and so on. The second part aids in determining whether the usual responses of individuals to stress are effective or ineffective. The third clarifies how individuals' resources for coping with stress are being utilized.

To take the Inventory, the individual is advised to seek out a quiet place where there will be no distractions for an hour or more. Part A lists the roles individuals usually play and includes blank spaces that can be filled in with the person's other roles. First of all, the individual checks off the roles he or she carries out and estimates the degree of stress characteristic of each. Impending role changes are included. If a person

*The Inventory is at the end of this chapter.

expects to change jobs, for example, the present and the new jobs would both be listed. Estimating the degree of stress associated with a role is, of course, a complex judgment.

On Part A of the Inventory the individual rates the overall stress of each role on a five-point scale:

5. Very high
4. Somewhat high
3. Moderate
2. Low
1. Very low

Both severity and pervasiveness of stress in the role should be taken into account. Liking for a role should not be confused with absence of stress. Liking may ameliorate stress somewhat, although not always. However, it by no means indicates a low level of stress as a consequence of the role. On the other hand, dislike of a role is likely to be indicative of stress. Even here, however, dislike of one role may be displacement of dislike of another role. It is important to insure that one evaluates accurately roles that in an undramatic way may be quite stressful; undemanding and boring roles are examples.

A rating of five should be given to any role that is stressful to the point of being intolerable, especially if that extends over more than a very short period. A rating of four is assigned to roles that are highly stressful yet tolerable or, if intolerable, where stress is experienced only periodically for short periods. A rating of three means that the role is stressful but quite manageable. Ratings of two and one apply to still lesser degrees of stress.

A role with a rating of five is, of course, cause for concern. So are two or more roles with ratings of four. If ratings of five and four total 14 or more, the individual very likely has a potentially disastrous role stress problem. If ratings of five and four total 10 to 13, the individual probably has a less severe but yet serious stress problem.

The individual then rates, also on Part A of the Inventory, the main sources of stress of roles with ratings of five or four (or of roles with lower ratings if the individual has reason to improve coping effectiveness with those). Sources of stress are as outlined in the preceding chapters: conflict within a role, conflict between two or more of a person's roles, conflict between a person's role and the role of another person, overdemand, underdemand, restrictiveness, role loss, taking on new roles, rejection, and encroachment.

The individual checks those that are important sources of stress in regard to the role in question. Usually one or only a few are checked. Often a good deal of thought is required, however, to determine the main sources of stress. If conflict between roles is checked, then the individual notes on the form which other role or roles, carried out by him or her or by another person, are involved. More specific sources of stress are noted by the individual. What, for example, are the kinds of overdemand that are most stressful? Which dimensions of the role are in conflict with one another or with which dimensions of which other roles are they in conflict?

Part B of the Inventory concerns the effectiveness or ineffectiveness of the responses the individual typically uses in coping with stress in the given role. The responses are those discussed in Chapter Three: aggression, self-destruction, distortion, overconformity, withdrawal, physical illness, and innovation. For example, in coping with the work role, which responses does the individual typically use if the source of stress is conflict with family roles? If it is overdemand in the work role? Using the following five-point scale, in general how effective or ineffective is the given response in counteracting the negative effects of the source of stress?

5. Very effective
4. Somewhat effective
3. Neither effective nor ineffective
2. Somewhat ineffective
1. Very ineffective

Part C of the Inventory has to do with the resources the individual typically draws upon in coping with problems in a given stressful role and whether those resources are being utilized effectively. Resources are classified as time, energy, money, material goods, influence, and friends. Other resources are filled in by the individual—for example, psychiatric counseling. Ratings for each resource are made by the individual as to availability, extent of allocation to the role, overutilization, underutilization, and effectiveness.

USE OF THE INVENTORY

The sheer fact of completing the Inventory requires that the individual think about his or her role stress problems in a systematic way. It pinpoints the main roles that are causing stress, what the specific sources of stress are, which responses are typically effective or ineffective, and how resources are being utilized. This type of analysis is the first and critical step in reducing stress. The next step for the individual under stress is to decide on a plan of action. If more than one role is especially stressful, the decision must be made whether to give priority to one role over another or to devise a plan that deals with problems in two or more roles simultaneously. Usually it is best to emphasize one role at a time. The exception is when two of a person's roles are so intertwined that sensibly they must be treated together. (The working mother and the man with two jobs are ready examples.)

If the individual is faced with considerable or greater stress in two roles that are not closely intertwined, the decision must be made as to which should be given first priority. If a role is so stressful as to be absolutely intolerable, then that role must be given priority. However, if an individual is faced with high but not intolerable levels of stress in two roles, a choice as to priority will need to be made. Other things being equal, the role that is the less stressful of the two may well be given priority. The reason is that practice in coping with this role problem can be invaluable in coping effectively with the more severe role problem later.

REMOVAL FROM THE PROBLEM

The first necessity for the individual in developing a plan of action is to put some distance between himself or herself and the role problem. A workable plan is much more likely to evolve when one is not squarely in the midst of the stress situation. With distance comes perspective. Arranging a quiet weekend away may be possible. Even half a day by oneself in the car in the country can be sufficient. Having achieved some distance from the stress problem, the individual reviews the completed Role Stress Inventory. What are the main sources of stress? Should the plan emphasize modifying a role? Dropping a role? Replacing one role with another? Certain coping responses rather than others? Reallocating resources?

Next is a brainstorming session. The individual jots down any ideas for reducing stress that come to him or her. The first five solutions that come to mind are written down, no matter how far-fetched they may be. The aim is to get the mind loosened up and to create a set for innovatively hitting upon possible paths to solution. The person goes on to list all possible solutions that come to mind. Then the whole matter is set aside for a time. The individual engages in some pleasant but not especially demanding task or leisure activity and lets the subconscious work on the problem.

The individual again concentrates on the problem, reviews the notes of the previous session. What other possible solutions come to mind? Those are added to the list. The mind is allowed to wander over key elements in the role situation that might be recombined with each other or combined with some condition or element not now in the situation in a new way. One cannot force the innovative process. However, once having analyzed the problem and having considered a variety of possible solutions, an innovative idea may come, as long as one does not try to force it.

DECIDING ON A COPING PLAN

All the possible solutions that have been listed in the two sessions are grouped into three categories as to the probability of success: good, moderate, or low. Those in the low category are discarded. The negative, as well as the positive consequences of each of the remaining proposed solutions, are considered. While an idea may be quite workable in one respect, is it likely to affect other aspects of one's life, other roles, negatively?

The three most feasible solutions are chosen. Then they are ranked in one, two, three order. The whole matter is dropped once again and the individual engages in some quite different activity. Then, returning once again to the role problem, all notes are reviewed. Are the three top solutions still the most feasible ones? Have other possibilities occurred to the individual? Finally, the solution most likely to be effective is chosen.

It will never be ideal. It will be that which promises the most benefits relative to costs.

PUTTING THE PLAN INTO ACTION

The individual next decides *how* to put the approach ranked first into action. When should one begin? Where? Should the change be instituted gradually or abruptly? Should one tell others first, explain at length, or say nothing? The individual attempts to imagine each step of the plan as it will actually be put into practice. What happens that tends to block progress that can be avoided when the real changes are actually made? Specific problems to be avoided or anticipated and ways of handling them are noted. If the individual finds that there appear to be too many unavoidable problems, he or she turns to the solution ranked second on the list. The steps of putting that into practice are imagined.

Next, the individual starts to actually carry out the plan. He or she should keep in mind the general idea of what is to be done and how. Not every detail should be planned. The eye should be kept on the ultimate goal. There should be flexibility about the steps along the way. Persistence without rigidity is important.

MONITORING

The individual monitors the success of the proposed solution. A diary is kept of what actions are taken and of the results. In what ways is the plan working well? Poorly? How much of the time? Is it causing serious negative consequences? Is one comfortable with it? The plan should be given ample time to get results. If it appears to be working, the individual continues to monitor its effectiveness. The diary is kept up and reviewed. Often, from the diary notes, a clear picture emerges of which specific actions have led to success, which to failure. The one can be emphasized, the other de-emphasized.

When it appears that the plan may have been effective, careful evaluation is made of the whole change process. Have the changes made clearly had the desired results? Has stress been reduced significantly? In

The Role Stress Inventory—Part A

Role	Overall Stress	Conflict within the Role	Conflict between Person's Roles [a]	Conflict between Person's Role & Roles of Others [a]	Over-demand	Under-demand	Restric-tiveness	Loss of Role	New Role	Rejec-tion	Encroach-ment
Sex											
Age											
Social Class											
Racial											
Ethnic											
Religious											
Husband or Wife											
Father or Mother											
Son or Daughter											
Grandparent											
Grandchild											
In-law:											

154

Housewife
Primary Job
Secondary Job

Student

Community
Organizations:
_____
_____
_____

Recreational:
_____
_____

Other:
_____
_____

5 = Very high.   3 = Moderate.   1 = Very low.
4 = Somewhat high. 2 = Low.

aSpecify other roles involved.

some respects and not in others? No outcome is likely to be perfect. Are the results acceptable? If not, the plan is revised. If the results are acceptable, in some cases it will be necessary to continue the remedy indefinitely. In others, once the remedy has brought the desired results, the plan should be set aside. One must know when to continue a successful plan and when to cease one.

ROLE CRISIS

If faced with an exceedingly stressful role crisis situation, then, the individual may have little choice but to deal with it immediately. It may not be possible to distance oneself from the problem in the way described earlier. The individual should, as far as feasible, follow the steps outlined above—but in compressed fashion. He or she gathers as much information about the problem as is possible in a very short time and then sits down somewhere where it is quiet. Some degree of relaxation will usually come by thinking about some one thing that is pleasant for a few minutes. Using the Role Stress Inventory on pages 154–158, diagnosis as to what is causing the problem is made. Then various solutions are considered in as flexible a manner as possible. They are written down. The individual attempts to take as impersonal a view of the crisis as possible. What would he or she advise someone else in that crisis situation to do? All possible solutions are written down. They are ranked.

The individual imagines putting the one ranked top into practice, keeping an eye out for negative consequences. He or she decides how to put the plan into action as decided. It is put into practice and its effectiveness is monitored. Alterations are made as necessary. There is further monitoring to determine when results have been achieved—that is, when the crisis has been ameliorated. Care is taken to allow for a period of gradual "running down" in the aftermath of the crisis. Just as a runner does not suddenly stop when he crosses the finish line, one should not suddenly relax when a crisis is passed. Some degree of involvement in another less stressful problem situation for a time is advisable. Otherwise, the resultant decompression can in itself be very stressful.

The Role Stress Inventory—Part B

Sources of stress	RESPONSES							
	Aggres-sion	Self-destruction	Dis-tortion	Over-conformity	With-drawal	Risk taking	Inno-vation	Physical illness

Examples
  Overdemand
    in Primary
    Work Roles
  Conflict
    between
    Person's
    Parental
    and Work Roles

_____

_____

_____

_____

_____

_____

5 = Very effective.   2 = Somewhat ineffective.
4 = Somewhat effective.   1 = Very ineffective.
3 = Neither effective nor ineffective.

The Role Stress Inventory—Part C

	RESOURCES				
	Availability	Extent of allocation	Over-utilization	Under-utilization	Effectiveness

Role ———————————

    Time
    Energy
    Money
    Material Goods
    Influence
    Friends
    Other

    —————————
    —————————
    ****

Role ———————————

    Time
    Energy
    Money
    Material Goods
    Influence
    Friends
    Other

    —————————
    ****

Role ———————————

    Time
    Energy
    Money
    Material Goods
    Influence
    Friends
    Other

    —————————
    —————————

5 = Very high.   3 = Moderate.   1 = Very low.
4 = Somewhat high. 2 = Somewhat low.

16

Planned Social Change

AVOIDING HAPHAZARD PLANNING

Individuals go through life meeting and attempting to cope with one role stress problem after another. They try to adapt to role stress. They try to change their roles. Sometimes their attempts are effective; often they are not. As we have seen, individuals can learn to improve their abilities for coping with role stress. However, that is but one side of the coin of change. Also needed is planned social change: carefully thought out programs for changing the essential character of roles, of role situations, of bureaucracy, and of the social institutions themselves.

Making work roles more satisfying for all, including mothers and the aged, probably would do more to extend the average length of life than any medical science breakthrough. Redesigning bureaucratic roles not only would free workers of terribly burdensome restrictions; it could make government services and industrial goods far more available at less cost. Modifying family roles in certain respects would have an enormous, positive impact on the mental health of society's members. Bringing about constructive change in the roles of students and teachers could lead to a revolution in learning, a revolution that would allow the human potential for innovation to flower far beyond anything now imaginable.

Creating social change in the direction desired is, of course, an extremely complex task. Very often not only do the desired goals elude us; in addition there may be unintended consequences that, on balance, lead to a larger problem than existed originally. Yet we have no choice but to be a part of social change. The world and societies within it change constantly or wither away. The choice is whether to make a conscious, concerted, coherent effort to effect change toward desired ends. We do this in some areas of life, in any case. In government and the economic sphere we constantly lay plans for change. Those plans may often go awry, but there is the emphasis on planned change. Such plans may not be looked upon as involving changes in social roles. Yet in one way or another most of them do. The conscious emphasis on social planning is not necessarily on role change, yet the implied outcome is a change in social roles. Affirmative action programs, for example, are basically designed to change the power relationships in sex, class, social, and ethnic roles.

The social institution that is most ignored in planned change is the family. This is considered the private preserve of individual citizens. Yet, viewed as a social institution, it is not that at all. The family is a complex system of social roles. Individuals are born into that system, and to a considerable degree most have to make do with their role heritage. A newcomer to this world can hardly be expected to redesign the roles of his or her family in childhood. By the time the person becomes an adult he or she is so formed by those roles, and stressed by them, that taking the initiative to induce change is, in practice, unlikely.

Of course, we are engaged in the business of bringing about change in family roles all the time. The current emphasis on women's liberation obviously involves this. The continuing attempts to change child rearing practices attest to it. So does concern with the aged. However, these changes are attempted in piecemeal fashion, each separate from the other. Yet they are inextricably related to one another and to the larger phenomenon of the family as a social institution. Hence, the necessity is to take a broad and comprehensive view of family roles and to articulate change in any one with change in the others.

FAMILY ROLES

For most adults the marital role is at the center of a complex constellation of roles. It is in the marital role that husband and wife seek support and solace in the face of stress—often severe, in other roles. Yet the marital role in the United States has itself become a stressful role. We have seen that being married is a tremendously effective antidote for stress. We also know that divorce is a very stressful process that impairs greatly individuals' abilities to cope with stress in other roles. In the United States, when marriages work, they usually work well. When they do not, and that is often, they can be damaging as well.

In a role relationship such as marriage, reciprocity—mutual support—is of paramount importance. Power must be evenly distributed if the relationship is to be beneficial for both partners. Yet in the United States presently, a central problem in the marital roles is the perceived power imbalance between husband and wife. "Perceived" is important, since part of the problem is one of perception of power. As the astute sociologist William I. Thomas said half a century ago, "When individuals perceive situations as real, then they are real in their consequences." When women perceive that wives are bereft of power in the marital relationship, then that relationship is cast in power terms, women feel deprived, and men are defensive.

Power takes many forms. We have had thousands of natural experiments in marriage as a set of role relationships over countless generations in hundreds of societies around the world. Hardly ever have wives held more explicit power than husbands. Yet as is well known, wives have often possessed much power in informal, indirect yet very real fashion. The idea of the woman as the power behind the throne has extended from royalty to poor agrarian families. In any case, the necessity is to remove contention and conflict from the marital roles rather than compound them. The adversarial relationship that is in these present times so commonly assumed to be a part of almost all human affairs has no place in marriage.

Parent and child roles clearly need reconsideration. Above all, the role of the parent is to be an affectionate guide to the child. The child needs love, warmth, and psychic as well as physical reward; he or she also needs guidance in learning to be a social human being. The child does not need to be coerced into following rules. Rather, the child needs help in learning how society works, what he or she is expected to do to become a functioning, contributing member of society, and how to do it. A child also needs a climate for being creative. Affectionate parents who act as guides to life are likely to provide that climate.

Too often parents are overdemanding or underdemanding in their expectations for their children. They tend to extremes, either to feel the child should measure up closely to minute rules of etiquette and of behavior generally or they ignore the child's behavior. This extremism is an outgrowth of the parents' bewilderment over how to be a parent, over what is expected of him or her as a parent. After all, parents are expected to be the primary persons responsible for the care and training of new members of the society. That is an awesome responsibility. Yet, as we know, it is almost impossible for parents and potential parents to gain training in how to meet those responsibilities. Thus, the parent—frustrated, confused, and ignorant—either may rigidly demand over-conformity on the part of the child in the hope of somehow blindly achieving at least a modicum of conformity or may ignore the whole matter. Some parents go toward one extreme, some toward the other, and some vacillate between the two.

One of the best pieces of advice to be given to parents is to avoid being overly concerned about what friends and neighbors will think of one as a parent. Rather, parents should be concerned about how the child can be helped to be a contributing, constructive adult who will feel a sense of reward from living out his or her life. To do this it is necessary to understand—at least to some moderate degree—the social system in which one lives, the nature of social roles, and the stresses that they can engender.

WORK ROLES

As discussed earlier, we very often concern ourselves with how individuals can be taught or otherwise brought to adjust more effectively to their work roles. Seldom do we give attention to how work roles should be reshaped, adjusted, or changed to cause workers less stress. Work roles are elements of the economy, and the economy is seen as a monolithic social system in many ways beyond the control of mortal men and women; it is this belief that makes it so.

Moderate levels of stress are necessary for healthy personal existences. Some stress in work roles helps to get work done. The challenge of moderately demanding work can be exhilarating. However, excessive levels of work stress, due either to conflict and overdemand or restriction and underdemand, are depressing and debilitating. They sap creativity and literally lead to early death. We need to have work accomplished in order for societies to survive. Yet we do not need to maim ourselves psychologically and weaken ourselves physically in the process.

From the point of view of planned social change, it will seldom do to redesign work roles solely at the work site. The effort to try to reshape a work role without changing somewhat the larger economic structures of which it is a part is almost always doomed to failure. The changes made in the role may seem to be effective for a while. In all likelihood, however, workers will soon be pretty much back where they were before. The work role may look a little different but the old, injurious stress levels will still be there. That will be because the larger configuration of economic roles and attitudes that surround the specific work roles have not changed.

The overriding necessities are to think in terms of changing the nature of the competitive process and the nature of bureaucracy. On the one hand, the severe competition that is part and parcel of life in the United States, especially in the economic realm, stresses individuals unduly by demanding too much and because of the conflict inherent in the competitive process. On the other hand, bureaucracy stresses individuals by placing excessive restrictions on them and often demanding too little otherwise.

We are all too prone to accept our competitive economic system as a given not to be changed. Similarly, we accept as virtually immutable the giant bureaucratic systems and the work roles that comprise them. We try to find ways of helping individuals adjust to intolerable work roles rather than try to bring about changes in the economy and bureaucracy that will allow work roles to be modified so that they are less stressful and far more rewarding.

Economic systems and bureaucracy are to serve humans, not the other way around. We have gotten this backwards. The need is to re-create a social system that allows human potential to flourish and that encourages creativity. The emphasis of bureaucracy on roles that demand narrowly conforming behavior, regardless of individual differences, must be shifted. The emphasis must be placed on the value rather than the liability of uniqueness in individuals. Excessive competitive conflict must be seen for what it is—a debilitating drain on human health and happiness. Unduly competitive roles must be replaced by those that emphasize the challenge of striving for goals without expectations that opponents must be overcome.

THE SCHOOLS

School systems have become bureaucratic systems. Teachers are interchangeable cogs in a teaching machine that results in very little learning. Twelve years of "processing" turns out student "products" who in far too many instances are alienated from the learning process. The urban schools in the main reflect typical bureaucratic conditions: rigid, restrictive, and otherwise undemanding roles for both students and teachers. Yet conflict between student and teacher roles often runs high. In many instances teachers are middle class, purveying middle class values to lower class, resentful students. Moreover, the teacher's role is to induce mental and behavioral conformity, while the student's natural inclinations are to explore, to express, to experiment, and to test boundaries.

There are, to be sure, exceptions. Grand exceptions. There are schools where student and teacher roles are flexible, allowing the innovative process to flourish. There are those rare schools where teachers are able to design course content much as they wish and to choose books that they deem suitable. Also, there are schools where students are encouraged to explore the world, to learn at their own pace, and to be creative. However, such schools are few and far between. Most are in affluent neighborhoods. The masses of children are in lock-step schools, often expending their energies in rebelling against rigid role demands.

Certainly, those rare schools that encourage innovation can serve as models for the development of schools and roles that do not hamstring permanently the mental and sometimes emotional processes of both students and teachers. Effective schools for upper middle class children cannot, of course, be transposed wholesale to lower class neighborhoods. Yet, while certain modifications are necessary, the basic conditions for encouraging and facilitating learning and creative endeavor are the same everywhere. The essential element is reward—rather than punishment—for learning to think, to solve problems, and to innovate.

A society can tolerate only so much innovation. This is where a fundamental problem arises in the education of the young. In our compulsive search to insure stable social organizations, we have become overly fearful of innovation and creativity, especially in children. We stamp it out by attempting to strait jacket them in rigid student roles. The unspoken assumption is that if we make individuals sufficiently role bound early enough in life they will not threaten the social organization with too many new ideas later. This is at once true and false. Children subjected to twelve years of typical student role demands are unlikely later to flood the culture to the breaking point with constructive, innovative ideas. However, they are likely—all too likely—to become rebels whose central cause is to tear down the social structure.

THE ADVERSARIAL SOCIETY

We are fast becoming an adversarial society. This is one of the great dangers that we face as a people. Many of us have come to believe, in a fundamental way, that competition is an inevitable component of human relationships. We espouse cooperation, helping, and "caring." However, the ways we construe and act out our relationships and the expectations we hold for one another's roles belie that. A major reason for the present unspoken emphasis on adversarial roles in everyday life is the generally competitive nature of our society. We compete fiercely for success goals of money, prestige, material goods, and power—that is, economic and class roles cost individuals in basic contentious and conflicted relationships. This is carried over as "normal" to other areas of life.

Thus the marital roles are increasingly seen as adversarial. If one spouse gains, the other supposedly loses. Parent-child roles are similarly construed. Students and teachers are assumed to be locked in conflict because of divergent pursuits, rather than both being cast as engaged in the same processes of learning and innovating. Police and citizenry, government officials and populace, the press and the politicians, and countless others are seen as adversaries.

Negotiation, which always implies adversarial roles, is viewed as a paramount process in all human relations. Citizens' interest groups form around countless issues. Much of life is cast in terms of power relationships. The point is not that these constructions of everyday life are totally in error. ather, the problem lies in their exaggeration as part and parcel of existence. Power, adversarial relations, negotiation, confrontation—these always have been, and no doubt changes will be threaded through human affairs. But not through all aspects of life. Husband and wife, mother and child, student and teacher, friend and friend—these are relationships that are often most rewarding and constructive precisely because power and negotiation are not at issue.

It is the sense of genuine *reciprocity* that needs to be brought back into role relationships in United States society. This means developing expectations that individuals will help one another carry out their roles rather than negotiate not to hinder each other. It means placing a clear emphasis on cooperative rather than competitive role playing. What we do by the present fixation with adversarial relationships and confrontation is to cast roles in conflict with one another where there was little or no conflict; where there already was conflict between individuals' roles, conflict is heightened by this self-fulfilling emphasis.

At the same time, a slavish devotion to excessive cooperation in human relationships can be abortive and ultimately stressful. Too great an emphasis on cooperation leads to restrictive roles. For excessive cooperation demands that everyone be in a niche, carefully following closely scripted roles in order to be fully predictable. The zestful challenge of some unpredictability, of some competition, and of striving to accomplish goals is missing. Thus, excessive cooperation means excessive conformity. It leads to the stamping out of creativity and the stultifying consequences of boredom.

17

Coping with the Future

THE SHAPE OF THE FUTURE

The shape of the future is, of course, in certain respects impossible to discern. However, in others the broad outlines of social life are clear. Social change will become increasingly rapid. This includes change in the fundamental nature of various social roles, especially familial and work roles. Machines and humans will interact to a greater and greater extent. More by far than in the past, significant "others" will, for a given person, be machines as well as men and women. Societies will at once become more impersonal and more personal. The present trend to mass society will increase in the sense that countries will combine into larger political units. At the same time, the present emphasis on local autonomy at the neighborhood level will decidedly increase. There will be more attention paid to and more value placed on human diversity.

The last is a happy prospect. It is dictated by the broad social changes that are sweeping the globe. As machines take over the bureaucratic and other routine tasks, it will become increasingly apparent that in the realm of work humans are needed only as high level specialists in economic, governmental, and educational activities. Intellectual specialization necessarily rewards human diversity. Humans will gradually become the select caste of high level planners and policy makers who direct the armies of machines that carry out the tasks now undertaken by the masses of men and women.

Much of this work by humans will, as Alvin Toffler suggests, be done in the home at electronic work benches: the "electronic cottage" in Toffler's phrase. This will mean greater integration of family and work roles. Also, especially noteworthy, it will mean that children come once again, as they did in the craftsman's home and the farmhouse, to know the meaning of work.

We will be far healthier—much less disease ridden. We will live 25 to 30 years longer on the average. However, that will apply to the world 100 years from now. For those of us presently attempting to cope with everyday life, what do the next 25 or 50 years hold? A period of transition to the new world is already underway. The signs of it are everywhere. The energy crisis is but one glaring symbol of the dislocations that come with transition and the onset of rapid change. The divorce rate of 50 percent (half of the new marriages in the United States end in divorce) is another symptom of dislocation. We are going to have to cope with rapidly accelerating social change in a future whose specific characteristics are, in many instances, far from clear.

What does this mean in regard to the roles we play, role stress, and coping with role stress? The most obvious point is that we must prepare for, grow accustomed to, our roles changing more rapidly than in the past. Given roles will, in many instances, be quite different than we had expected them to be. This will be true not only for family and work roles. Community roles, class roles, school roles, and others will shift in ways not anticipated. As to class, for example, the energy crisis affects very much the moderately well-to-do upper middle class as well as the lower class. Being a mother, being a teacher, being a doctor, being an aged person, being an upper middle class person—all of these roles will change much more in the next 30 years than they have in the past 100 years.

Rapid change in the expectations for roles means uncertainty, insecurity, and anxiety. It can lead to conflict—conflict between the older versions of the role and the new versions and conflict between a given changing role and another changing role because of lack of clarity as to how the two are integrated with each other. Also, it obviously can lead to a certain form of overdemand that arises out of expectations that the individual adjust to rapidly shifting role conditions. For some, of course, this can be a rewarding challenge rather than an onerous overdemand.

The constructive challenge that is inherent in the "new world" is not to be overlooked. While some will find the gap between what was expected of one and what is to be expected a source of harrowing frustration, others will find in it enormous satisfaction. The humdrum quality of life occasioned by undemanding, restrictive roles will for many be replaced by daily challenges that in their solution provide continual reward. Others of us will be trapped in webs of expectations that coerce us to be one-dimensional machines even more than at present. This will be due to the great uncertainty over the role of the machine versus the role of the human worker in the transition period of the next twenty-five to fifty years.

The next decades hold, then, the dual promises of widening opportunities for the expression of creative talents and of widening restrictions on individual behavior and proclivity. There seems little doubt that some will be far better off and others far worse off in regard to role stress and its effects. Of one thing we can be certain. Unlike the past and present, substantial concern will be given to the phenomenon of role stress. What causes it, how to cope with it, how to bring about planned change that reduces it—these will receive enormously increased attention.

THE FUTURE OF THE SEX ROLES

Clearly, women in the United States will continue to move into roles previously held largely by men. This applies not only to the realm of work. Women will participate as never before in leadership roles in the community, in religion, and in government. To a lesser degree, men will follow the trend already begun of taking on work roles traditionally filled by women: nursing, elementary school teaching, and secretarial work are examples. Men will spend more time as "househusbands."

The nature of these roles—once the province of one sex and in the future increasingly of both—will change. So, too, will the sex roles of male and female per se. One can expect the sex roles to converge to some degree. Female roles will, in all likelihood, take on greater elements of competition and aggression, while male roles will have less of those. Similarly, the stressful nature of roles carried out in the past mainly by men, especially work roles, should lessen somewhat. Also, to the extent that women's work and other roles have not been especially stressful, they can be expected to become more so. Overall, it is reasonable to foresee that the roles males hold will become less stressful and those that women hold will become more stressful.

It should be no surprise, then, if in the decades ahead women increasingly experience more severe symptoms of stress, while male symptoms decrease. Death rates due to heart disease may, for example, very well rise for females and decline for males. The same should be true of death rates due to accidents and suicide. As for mental illness, one would expect rates of psychosis to rise for females and fall for males.

At least some social scientists who analyze changes in women's roles are persuaded that this will not be so. They see females as somehow coping effectively with the stresses of their new roles. They reason that the ways women have coped with role problems in the past will stand them in good stead in the future. This seems a somewhat overly optimistic view. More likely, two broad classes of women will continue to develop: the traditionalists and the competitors. The first emphasizes the role of homemaker, which is relatively immune to a rise in stress symptomatology. For them stress may well decrease because of the sensible changes in the housewife's role that are making it less restrictive and more rewarding. For the competitors, in competition with men, the symptoms of stress may well rise to rates at least as high as those of males in recent decades. It is probably true that the roles that women will move into, roles that were in the past largely held by men, will be somewhat less stressful than heretofore. Nevertheless, they will tend to be stressful especially in the areas of overdemand and conflict. Women will not have received the informal stress training in the course of everyday life that their male counterparts have received. Even that training has not allowed men to cope especially effectively with stress. Competitive women may very well be psychologically unprepared for the roles to which they so strongly aspire.

THE FAMILY

As we move through the pronounced social changes of the next decades, family roles are likely to become less conflicted on the one hand and less restrictive on the other. The family will probably play a greater part as a support system for coping with change in the wider society. In times of adversity the family gains in strength and durability. Much of the subordinate-superior dimension of the role relationship between child and parents should wither and be replaced by constructive cooperation. As noted, work will be done in the home to a greater and greater extent. Children and parents will work together toward common goals.

Contention and violence in the family can thus be expected to decrease. The time may not be far off when physical violence between spouses, between siblings, and between parents and children will be seen as an anachronistic perversion. While psychological violence will perhaps decrease somewhat, the process will in all likelihood be much slower than in the case of physical violence. Psychological violence can take almost limitless indirect and not readily discernible forms. Despite the rise of the family as a support system, the tensions produced by change in the broader social environment will continue to lead to the veiled venting of aggression within the family. An important necessity here is for family members to realize that the family is, as in many societies it has always been, an escape valve for the aggressive tensions members generate in response to outside frustration. Individuals would do well to face this fact squarely. If, up to a point, they accept one another's anger, they provide mutual support. Recognition that the role relationships of family members involve elements of psychological aggression takes the onus off individuals both as perpetrators and as victims. That is, acceptance of the fact that within the family we sometimes need to vent hostility to remain healthy, because it cannot be vented elsewhere without dire consequences, can be salutary for all. This is not a notion that is likely to be popular, but it contains a strong dose of realism.

SCHOOL ROLES

As we pass through the age of uncertainty about the roles of humans in relation to those of machines, a two-track system in the education of the young seems likely unless we take definite steps to prevent it. Far more than at present, the schools of the near future may well be designed to manufacture either drones or thinkers. The drones will be trained to do those routine tasks that cannot yet conveniently be done by machines. The thinkers will be free to innovate as to how the machines and drones should be employed.

To be sure, there has for generations existed—in a fundamental sense—this drone-thinker dichotomy in our lower schools. The poor learn—if badly—the basic reading, writing, and arithmetic skills and may learn a "trade" in vocational school. The well-to-do go to the private schools and colleges and learn to be managers and professionals. The time will come when all young people are educated as thinkers. The machines will by then have taken over the roles of the drones and there will be no need for the latter. But that is in the long-range future. The next decades will very likely see an increasing division of the young into tracks that gear them for extremely restrictive work roles or for liberating, creative work roles.

For many, the drone role may well turn out to be especially compelling in an illusory way. It will promise security. If one goes through the training process adequately, one will be assured of a moderate income job for thirty years and then of modest financial security until death. The creative thinkers will have to take their chances. They will have the opportunities of large financial gain and high status. Those who fail will be consigned to wander in the purgatory of work relief. This, certainly, is not unlike the present work system; yet there will in all likelihood be far greater emphasis on routinization and security on the one hand and innovation and risk on the other.

Curricula for drones will emphasize the easy learning of recordings played under the pillow during sleep, of fun and games with the computer, or of feedback learning machines that guide the student unerringly toward highly predictable work behavior. Curricula for thinkers will stress strong rewards for effective problem solving of any kind. There will be ample opportunity for student thinkers to program the learning machines of drones and observe the results on television screens.

FURTHER IMPENDING CHANGE

We can expect to see a much greater questioning of the utility of prestige roles than at present or in the past. We are an invidious society, as are most others. We are forever ranking people as to worth. We dispense prestige as reward for work well done. We become fixated with social standing. This pits individual against individual in a never ending competition for false status. False because in the end status depends on minor differences in certain narrowly defined abilities that obscure the far greater abilities of all of us.

Individuals need not be ranked vertically, some higher and some lower, in order to distinguish among and to reward them. Horizontal distinctions emphasize equal worth and standing while they take into account individual differences. Rewards for work well done can be cast in terms of leisure and personal satisfaction that do not depend on money, prestige, and its material symbols.

This connects with the changes we can expect to see in future years regarding the nature, meaning, and evaluation of human achievements. In many "modern" societies, achievement has been measured in terms of power. This, in turn, has been measured by economic output. The person who can produce more, who can produce the machines that produce more, or who can generate the ideas that can lead to the production of those machines has been venerated. That is, work efficiency has been equated with power that has, in turn, been equated with achievement. Some of this will remain. However, greater emphasis may very well be given to the achievement of abstract ideas. Those who innovate ways of living more constructively are likely to be seen as high achievers, although those ways of living have less to do with power and more to do with that nebulous concept, happiness.

Accordingly, and as we are already witnessing, the social and behavioral sciences will be on the ascendency, while technology—including, and very importantly so, medical technology—will wane. The more rapid is social change in general and the shift from humans to machines in particular, the greater the need for the guidance that is inherent in sociology, psychology, cultural anthropology, and other social and behavioral sciences. It is only when a body of knowledge is truly necessary that we recognize it as fully legitimate and turn to it. With the great speed-up in social change, that time has come for those sciences, for what they offer is perhaps the most effective avenue to managing

173

and directing change and, to the extent necessary, to adjusting to it. Medicine can in almost no way do this. In relation to change, medicine can at best respond to the debilitating results of stress that can ensue from change, and then it is centrally an after-the-fact response—not a preventive one.

The decentralization of bureaucracy is likely to be a further theme of the future. Already underway, economic, governmental, and educational bureaucracies are changing such that the smaller units within them take on greater autonomy in planning, decision making, and everyday operations. With the advent of mass industrial society, we swung away from the preeminence of the primary group and toward "control from the top." We placed heavy emphasis on impersonal work roles. This served, in some degree, as a way of coping with the unknown consequences of emerging industrialization. However, as has been stressed in previous chapters, that was at the expense of individual expression and creativity. It was also at the expense of those local interpersonal controls—social disapproval and the like—so vital to a society's fundamental organization. We can expect, then, to see local planning committees take on increasingly dominant parts in their own destinies. As is already clearly evident, a wide variety of community roles for managing social change will evolve and proliferate.

Finally, the mass media are fast becoming the connectors between those semiautonomous local community units. Information and social values are shared by communities in large societies in considerable measure through television, radio, newspapers, and magazines. This trend will no doubt continue. National identities and personal identities as well, will increasingly depend on the overarching sense of community that instant and mass dissemination of facts, ideas, and values makes possible.

There are, in these ongoing or impending dimensions of social change, the seeds for personal liberation from the bondage that has come from being shackled by overdemanding roles, from being torn by conflicted roles, and from being depressed by undemanding and restrictive roles. The time of conscious control over our social lives through the rational design of our roles may well be at hand. Whatever we can do to hasten this transformation is likely to be beneficial.

References

CHAPTER 1: THE POWER OF ROLES

Defining Roles: For a classic definition, see Ralph Linton, *The Study of Man*, New York: Appleton-Century-Crofts, 1936. The present author's *Deviance and Conformity: Roles, Situations, and Reciprocity*, New Haven, Conn.: College and University Press, 1970, is largely a role analysis of social behavior.

Learning Roles: For a good discussion of the socialization process, see Albert D. Ullman, *Sociocultural Foundations of Personality*, Boston: Houghton Mifflin, 1965.

Deviant Roles: An interesting analysis of deviant work roles is found in Gale Miller, *Odd Jobs: The World of Deviant Work*, Englewood Cliffs, N.J.: Prentice-Hall, 1978. On learning deviant roles, see Edwin M. Lemert, *Human Deviance, Social Problems, and Social Control*, Englewood Cliffs, N.J.: Prentice-Hall, 1967.

175

CHAPTER 2: ROLE STRESS

The Meaning of Role Stress: The classic statement on stress is Hans Selye, *The Stress of Life*, New York: McGraw-Hill, 1956. Also Sol Levine and Norman A. Scotch, *Social Stress*, Chicago: Aldine, 1970; Aaron Antonovsky, *Health, Stress, and Coping*, San Francisco: Jossey-Bass, 1979. For a layman's account, see Walter McQuade and Ann Aikman, *Stress*, New York: Dutton, 1974. For heart disease and stress, see James J. Lynch, *The Broken Heart*, New York: Basic Books, 1977.

Sources of Role Stress: The examples and generalizations made here are documented in references for Chapters 7–13.

Role Stress as Social Control: Edwin M. Lemert, *Human Deviance, Social Problems, and Social Control*, Englewood Cliffs, N.J.: Prentice-Hall, 1967. This conception is implicit in Robin H. Lauer, *Social Problems and the Quality of Life*, Dubuque, Iowa: William C. Brown, 1978; Alex Thio, *Deviant Behavior*, Boston: Houghton Mifflin, 1978; and Stuart Palmer, *Deviance and Conformity: Roles, Situations, and Reciprocity*, New Haven, Conn.: College and University Press, 1970.

CHAPTER 3: RESPONSES TO ROLE STRESS

Aggression toward Others: Leonard Berkowitz, *Aggression: A Social Psychological Analysis*, New York: McGraw-Hill, 1962.

Self-Destructive Behavior: Gene Lester and David Lester, *Suicide: The Gamble with Death*, Englewood Cliffs, N.J.: Prentice-Hall, 1971.

Distortion: Aaron Antonovsky, *Health, Stress, and Coping*, San Francisco: Jossey-Bass, 1979.

Withdrawal: Theodore Lidz and others, *Schizophrenia and the Family*, New York: International Universities Press, 1965.

Compulsive Conformity: On ritualism, see Robert K. Merton, "Social Structure and Anomie," in *Social Theory and Social Structure*, Glencoe, Ill.: Free Press, 1957, pp. 131–160.

Risk Taking: Samuel Z. Klausner, *Why Man Takes Chances*, New York: Doubleday, Anchor Books, 1968.

Physical Illness: Hans Selye, *The Stress of Life*, New York: McGraw-Hill, 1956; James J. Lynch, *The Broken Heart*, New York: Basic Books, 1977.

Innovation: Rollo May, *The Courage to Create*, New York: W. W. Norton & Co., Inc., 1975.

CHAPTER 4: PRESTIGE AND OCCUPATIONAL ROLES

Alexander Leaf, *Youth in Old Age*, New York: McGraw-Hill, 1975; James J. Lynch, *The Broken Heart*, New York: Basic Books, 1977; Meyer Friedman and Ray H. Rosenman, *Type A Behavior and Your Heart*, New York: Knopf, 1974.

Prestige Roles: The Guralnick Report, cited in Table 4.1, is one of the few broadscale analyses of death from specific causes by occupation in the United States: Lillian Guralnick, *Mortality by Occupation and Cause of Death among Men 20 to 64 Years of Age: United States, 1950*, Washington, D.C.: U.S. Department of Health, Education and Welfare, Vital Statistics–Special Reports, vol. 53, no. 3, September 1963. Regarding average length of life for blacks and whites in the United States, see *Statistical Abstract of the United States*, 1977, Washington, D.C.: U.S. Government Printing Office, 1977, p. 65.

Occupational Roles: The Tennessee study of occupational mortality is concerned with that state only but includes males as well as females: National Institute for Occupational Safety and Health, *Proceedings of Occupational Stress Conference*, Washington, D.C.: U.S. Government Printing Office, no date (approximately 1978). The study mentioned at the end of the chapter regarding high death rates among young women physicians is cited in Barbara Ehrenreich, "Is Success Dangerous to Your Health?" *Ms. Magazine*, May 1978.

CHAPTER 5: SEX ROLES AND MARRIAGE

Male and Female Roles: England is an example of a society where females are more prone than males to kill their own children. The data on female life expectancy and female overall death rates compared to those for males in the United States are from *Statistical Abstract of the United States*, 1977, Washington, D.C.: U.S. Government Printing Office, 1977, pp. 25 and 68. The figures on the likelihood of U.S. males dying of cardiovascular-renal disease and malignant neoplasms as compared to females are from Evelyn M. Kitagawa and Philip M. Hauser, *Differential Mortality in the United States: A Study in Socioeconomic Epidemiology*, Cambridge, Mass.: Harvard University Press, p. 88. The data on male and female suicide and homicide victimization are from *Statistical Abstract of the United States, 1977*, op. cit., p. 174. The reference to Types A and B personalities are from Meyer Friedman and Ray H. Rosenman, *Type A Behavior and Your Heart*, New York: Knopf, 1974. That women report symptoms of illness and use medical facilities more than men is documented in C. A. Nathanson, "Illness and the Feminine Role: A Theoretical Review," *Social Science and Medicine*, February 1975, vol. 9, pp. 57–62. For the higher rate of depressive disorders in women than men, see Bruce P. Dohrenwend, "Sociocultural and Social Psychological Factors in the Genesis of Mental Disorders," *Journal of Health and Social Behavior*, December 1975, vol. 16, pp. 365–392.

Marital Roles: The death rates by marital status are from Kitagawa and Hauser, op. cit., pp. 109–110. The reference for death rates of smokers and nonsmokers by marital status is Harold J. Morowitz, "Hiding in the Hammond Report," *Hospital Practice*, August 1975, pp. 35–39. The U.S. death rates from coronary heart disease and hypertensive disease for persons aged 35 to 44 years by marital status are from James J. Lynch, *The Broken Heart*, New York: Basic Books, 1977, Appendix, Tables B-8 and B-9. The table headed "Ratio of Death Rates of Widowed to Married Persons for Coronary Heart Disease, United States, 1959–1961" is from the same source, p. 51. So are the data on death rates due to cancer that immediately follow that table (Lynch, pp. 44 and 242). However, the figures in the table headed "Death Rates for Divorced, Widowed, and Single as Percent of Death Rate for Married White Males, Aged 15 to 64 Years, Standardized for Age, United States, 1959–1961" are taken from Hugh Carter and Paul C. Glick, *Marriage and Divorce: A Social and Economic Study*, Cambridge, Mass.: Harvard University Press, 1976, p. 346. The suicide and homicide victimization rates that follow that table are from the same source, p. 345. The source for the data on death rates due to accidents at the end of this chapter is Albert P. Iskant and Paul V. Joliet, *Accidents and Homicide*, Cambridge, Mass.: Harvard University Press, 1968, pp. 139 and 151. The final statement regarding motor vehicle fatalities is based on the work of David P. Phillips, "Suicide, Motor Vehicle Fatalities, and the Mass Media: Evidence toward a Theory of

Suggestion," paper presented at annual meeting of the American Sociological Association, San Francisco, August 1978.

CHAPTER 6: ROLE STRESS IN THE UNITED STATES AND THE WORLD

Two Extremes: Nevada and Utah: The data in the first two paragraphs are from Victor Fuchs, *Who Shall Live?*, New York: Basic Books, 1974, pp. 52–54, except the crime statistics at the end of the second paragraph that are from the U.S. Federal Bureau of Investigation, *Crime in the United States, 1977*, Washington, D.C.: U.S. Government Printing Office, 1978. The "average lifetime" data in paragraph three are from *Statistical Abstract of the United States, 1976*, Washington, D.C.: U.S. Government Printing Office, 1976, p. 59. The infant mortality rates in paragraph four are from p. 64 of the same source, while the other death rates in that paragraph are from Fuchs, op. cit., pp. 52–54. Homicide rates in paragraph five are taken from *Statistical Abstract . . .* , op. cit., p. 54.

    The States of the U.S.: The book referred to at the outset is David L. Dodge and Walter T. Martin, *Social Stress and Chronic Illness*, Notre Dame, Ind.: University of Notre Dame Press, 1970. The correlation between death rates and three indicators of socioeconomic levels are from Evelyn M. Kitagawa and Philip M. Hauser, *Differential Mortality in the United States*, Cambridge, Mass.: Harvard University Press, 1973.

    Countries around the World: The source for the death rates in paragraph two is James J. Lynch, *The Broken Heart*, New York: Basic Books, 1977, p. 31. Life expectancies for various countries around the globe are from *Statistical Abstract . . .* , op. cit., p. 895.

CHAPTER 7: CONFLICT WITHIN A ROLE

The Problem: On double bind, see Gregory Bateson and others, "Toward a Theory of Schizophrenia," *Behavioral Science*, vol. 1, pp. 251–264. On role problems, Bruce J. Biddle and Edwin J. Thomas, eds., *Role Theory: Concepts and Research*, New York: John Wiley, 1966.

    The Foreman: Thomas H. Patten, *The Foreman: Forgotten Man of Man-*

agement, New York: American Management Association, 1968. Charles R. Walker and others, *The Foreman on the Assembly Line*, Cambridge, Mass.: Harvard University Press, 1956. The Tennessee Study: National Institute for Occupational Safety and Health, *Proceedings of Occupational Stress Conference*, Washington, D.C.: U. S. Government Printing Office, no date (approximately 1978).

The Waitress: William Foote Whyte, *Human Relations in the Restaurant Industry*, New York: McGraw-Hill, 1948.

The President: James D. Barber, *The Presidential Character*, Englewood Cliffs, N.J.: Prentice-Hall, 1972.

The Police Officer: Jeffrey A. Schwartz and Cynthia B. Schwartz, "The Personal Problems of the Police Officer: A Plea for Action," in William H. Kroes and Joseph J. Hurrell, Jr., eds., *Job Stress and the Police Officer: Identifying Stress Reduction Techniques*, Washington, D.C.: National Institute for Occupational Safety and Health, U.S. Department of Health, Education and Welfare, 1975, pp. 130–141. See, as well, other chapters in that volume. Also, Albert S. Reiss, Jr., *The Police and the Public*, New Haven: Yale University Press, 1972; and David J. Bordua, ed., *The Police: Six Sociological Essays*, New York: John Wiley, 1967.

CHAPTER 8: CONFLICT
BETWEEN ROLES

Working Mothers: William H. Chafe, *The American Woman: Her Changing Social, Economic, and Political Roles, 1920–1970*, New York: Oxford University Press, 1972.

The Physician: For an interesting consideration of the doctor and patient roles, Samuel W. Bloom, *The Doctor and His Patient*, New York: Free Press, 1963.

Conflict in Age Roles in Midlife: Daniel J. Levinson, *The Seasons of a Man's Life*, New York: Knopf, 1977; Gail Sheehy, *Passages*, New York: Dutton, 1974.

Conflict between Two Persons' Roles: On marital conflict, Sydney H. Croog and others, "Patterns of Marital Conflict," *Heart Patient Study: Report No. 7*, mimeo, 1969. Regarding humans and machines, see Rosemary Stewart, *How Computers Affect Management*, London: Macmillan, 1971; a basic work, recently reissued, is Norbert Wiener, *The Human Use of Human Beings*, New York: Avon, 1980.

CHAPTER 9: OVERDEMANDING ROLES

Overdemand Is Relative: Meyer Friedman and Ray H. Rosenman, *Type A Behavior and Your Heart*, New York: Knopf, 1974. For an interesting view of work styles in corporate life, see Michael Maccoby, *The Gamesman*, New York: Simon and Schuster, 1976. On work demands and aggression toward family members, Sydney H. Croog, "The Family as a Source of Stress," in Sol Levine and Norman A. Scotch, *Social Stress*, Chicago: Aldine, 1970, p. 36. In the last paragraph of this section, regarding job demands and high rates of mental disorder and alcoholism, see L. E. Hinkle, Jr., "Physical Health, Mental Health, and the Corporate Environment," in L. R. Salyes, ed., *Individualism and Big Business*, New York: McGraw-Hill, 1963, ch. 11; as to overdemanding jobs and heart disease, J. S. House, "Occupational Stress and Coronary Heart Disease: A Review and Theoretical Integration," *Journal of Health and Social Behavior*, March 1974, vol. 15, pp. 12–27; the study of heart disease among physicians, dentists, and lawyers is reported in Aubrey Kagan, "Epidemiology and Society, Stress and Disease," in L. Levi, ed., *Society, Stress, and Disease*, vol. 1, London: Oxford University Press, pp. 36–48. On air controllers, see Don Biggs, *Pressure Cooker*, New York: W. W. Norton & Co., Inc., 1979.

CHAPTER 10: UNDEMANDING AND RESTRICTIVE ROLES

On Boredom: Mihaly Czikszentmihalyi, *Beyond Boredom and Anxiety*, San Francisco, Calif.: Jossey-Bass, 1975.

Bureaucracy and Role Stress: Richard H. Hall, *Occupations and Social Structure*, Englewood Cliffs, N.J.: Prentice-Hall, 1975.

Individual Differences and Underdemand: On risk, Samuel Klausner, ed., *Why Man Takes Chances*, New York: Doubleday, 1968. The study of overdemand and underdemand in twenty-three occupations is: Robert

Kaplan and others, *Job Demands and Worker Health*, U.S. Public Health Service, Washington, D.C.: U.S. Government Printing Office, 1975.

Sudden Shifts in Role Demands: Stuart Palmer, *Deviance and Conformity: Roles, Situations, and Reciprocity*, New Haven, Conn.: College and University Press, 1970.

The Aged: Rena Smith Blau, *Old Age in a Changing Society*, New York: New Viewpoints, 1973.

Restrictive Roles: Harvey Braverman, *Labor and Monopoly Capital: The Degradation of Work in the Twentieth Century*, New York: Monthly Review Press, 1974. One of the best studies of the assembly line is Eli Chinoy, *American Workers and Their Dreams*, New York: Doubleday, 1955. On flexibility of the housewife's role, see S. R. Orden and M. B. Norman, "Working Wives and Marriage Happiness," *American Journal of Sociology*, Jan. 1969, vol. 74, pp. 392–407.

The Prison Inmate: Gresham M. Sykes, *The Society of Captives*, Princeton, N.J.: Princeton University Press, 1958.

Mass Hysteria in the Factory: The example is based on reporting in *The New York Times*, May 29, 1979, pp. C1–2.

CHAPTER 11: ROLE LOSS

Forms of Role Change and Loss: A good, general work for the nonprofessional reader is Mortimer R. Feinberg, *Leavetaking*, New York: Simon and Schuster, 1978.

The Trauma of Role Loss: On loss and consequent heart disease, see James J. Lynch, *The Broken Heart*, New York: Basic Books, 1977.

Measures of Stress Due to Role Loss: On the Holmes scale, see M. Masuda and T. H. Holmes, "Magnitude Estimations of Social Readjustment," *Journal of Psychosomatic Research*, 1967, vol. II, no. 2, pp. 219–225. On the Dohrenwend scale, see Barbara D. Dohrenwend and others, "Exemplification of a Method for Scaling Life Events: The PERI Life Events Scale," *Journal of Health and Social Behavior*, vol. 19, pp. 205–229. The table that gives coronary heart disease death rate ratios for white and black males by age and marital status is from Iwao Marijama and others, *Cardiovascular Disease in the United States*, Cambridge, Mass.: Harvard University Press, 1971, p. 2. The source for the Engel analysis of sudden death is George L. Engel, "Sudden and Rapid Death during

Psychological Stress: Folklore or Folk Wisdom?" *Annals of Internal Medicine*, vol. 74, 1971, pp. 771–782. The data on institutionalization in mental hospitals and prisons by marital status and sex are from Hugh Carter and Paul C. Glick, *Marriage and Divorce: A Social and Economic Study*, Cambridge, Mass.: Harvard University Press, 1976, p. 334. The studies mentioned at the end of this section are cited by James J. Lynch, *The Broken Heart*, op. cit.

Involuntary Loss of a Job: Harvey Brenner, "Estimating the Social Costs of National Economic Policy," Paper No. 5, Joint Economics Committee, Congress of the United States, October 26, 1977.

Unexpected Role Loss: Stuart Palmer, *Deviance and Conformity: Roles, Situations, and Reciprocity*, New Haven, Conn.: College and University Press, 1970.

CHAPTER 12: NEW ROLES

Measuring Stress in New Roles: The stressful event scales mentioned are by M. Masuda and T. H. Holmes, "Magnitude Estimations of Social Readjustment," *Journal of Psychosomatic Research*, 1967, vol. II, no. 2, pp. 219–225; Barbara Dohrenwend and others, "Exemplification of a Method for Scaling Life Events: The PERI Life Events Scale," *Journal of Health and Social Behavior*, vol. 19, pp. 205–229. The data on overall death rates for the foreign born in the United States are from Evelyn M. Kitagawa and Philip M. Hauser, *Differential Mortality in the United States: A Study in Socioeconomic Epidemiology*, Cambridge, Mass.: Harvard University Press, 1973, p. 105; those data on death rates from accidents among the foreign-born are from Albert P. Iskant and Paul V. Joliet, *Accidents and Homicide*, Cambridge, Mass.: Harvard University Press, 1968, p. 149. The source for the information on residential mobility of families is James J. Lynch, *The Broken Heart*, New York: Basic Books, 1977, p. 11. For data on coronary heart disease, lung cancer, and residential mobility, see John Cassell, "Physical Illness in Response to Stress," in Sol Levine and Norman A. Scotch, eds., *Social Stress*, Chicago: Aldine, 1970, pp. 196–197. For sources regarding the relationship between suicide and mental disorders and residential mobility see Jack P. Gibbs and Walter T. Martin, *Status Integration and Suicide*, Eugene, Ore.: University of Oregon Press, 1964, p. 205; and L. E. Hinkle, Jr., "Physical Health, Mental

Health, and the Corporate Environment," in L. R. Salyes, ed., *Individualism and Big Business*, New York: McGraw-Hill, 1963, ch. 11. On low-income residential mobility and emotional disturbance, see Marc Fried, "Effects of Social Change on Mental Health," *American Journal of Orthopsychiatry*, vol. 34, 1964, pp. 3–28. Much of the material in the last paragraph of this section is from Mortimer R. Feinberg, *Leavetaking*, New York: Simon and Schuster, 1978, pp. 61–68.

Marital and Parental Roles: The sources for the family violence data are: Murray A. Straus and others, *Behind Closed Doors: Violence in the American Family*, New York: Doubleday, 1980; and Murray A. Straus, "Family Patterns and Child Abuse in a Nationally Representative American Family," *Child Abuse and Neglect*, vol. 3, 1979, 213–225.

Problems of Success: Alfred J. Marrow, ed., *The Failure of Success*, New York: AMACOM, 1972.

Taking on New Roles: Feinberg, op. cit.

CHAPTER 13: ROLE REJECTION AND ENCROACHMENT

Three outstanding works are Kenneth Keniston, *All Our Children: The American Family under Pressure*, New York: Harcourt Brace Jovanovich, Inc., 1977; William Ryan, *Blaming the Victim*, New York: Random House, 1971; Richard Sennett and Jonathan Cobb, *The Hidden Injuries of Class*, New York: Random House, 1972. Aspects of a chapter by Jaco are relevant: E. Gartley Jaco, "Mental Illness in Response to Stress," in Sol Levine and Norman A. Scotch, *Social Stress*, Chicago: Aldine, 1970, pp. 210–227, especially p. 216.

CHAPTERS 14 THROUGH 17: ON COPING WITH ROLE STRESS

These chapters have to do with the coping process and do not require specific citation. Some useful general works are: Aaron Antonovsky, *Health, Stress, and Coping*, San Francisco: Jossey-Bass, 1979; Julius Fast, *Creative Coping*, New York: Morrow, 1976; Mortimer R. Feinberg and others, *Leavetaking*, New York: Simon and Schuster, 1978; Brewster

Ghiselin, ed., *The Creative Process*, New York: New American Library, 1952; Daniel J. Levinson and others, *The Seasons of a Man's Life*, New York: Knopf, 1978; Michael J. Mahoney, *Self-Change: Strategies for Solving Personal Problems*, New York: W. W. Norton & Co., Inc., 1979; Rollo May, *The Courage to Create*, New York: W. W. Norton & Co., Inc., 1975; Walter McQuade and Ann Aikman, *Stress*, New York: Dutton, 1975; Donald Norfolk: *The Stress Factor*, New York: Simon and Schuster, 1977; Hans Selye, *Stress Without Distress*, Philadelphia: Lippincott, 1974; David Viscott, *Risking*, New York: Simon and Schuster, 1977.

Index